THE CREDIT CONUNDRUM

PSYCHOLOGICAL PRINCIPLES OF PERSONAL FINANCE AND CREDIT MANAGEMENT

THE ULTIMATE GUIDE TO SUCCESSFUL PERSONAL FINANCE AND CREDIT MANAGEMENT

NAKEL NIKIEMA

TABLE OF CONTENTS

INTRODUCTION

Credit is not just for economic transactions; it's a phenomenon that influences and is influenced by consumer behavior, societal norms, and financial institutions. In this book, you'll dive into the relationship between psychology and credit, examining how we perceive, use, and manage credit. This book will offer an overview of the cognitive, emotional, and social factors that shape credit behavior.

But before we go into the psychological principles at play, let's take a moment to understand the credit system itself. Credit systems vary widely across different regions, each with its own regulations.

In North America, credit scores are the base of the financial system. These three-digit numbers dictate not only whether you can get a loan but also the interest rates you'll pay and even the jobs you can apply for. The US, in particular, depends on credit scores generated by agencies like FICO and VantageScore (Black, 2021). These scores are influenced by a variety of factors, including payment history, credit utilization, length of credit history, new credit inquiries, and the mix of credit types.

Europe presents a slightly different picture. While credit scores are still important, the system is less centralized. Countries like the UK have their own agencies, such as Experian, Equifax, and TransUnion, that generate credit scores (El Issa, 2024). In contrast, some European countries rely more on banking history and less on a standardized credit-scoring system. For instance, Germany uses the Schufa system, which focuses on a person's payment history and outstanding debts.

Meanwhile, in emerging markets, the credit system is often in its nascent stages. Countries in Asia and Africa are increasingly adopting credit-scoring mechanisms, but many still depend on traditional banking relationships and informal credit assessments (World Bank Group, 2019). The rapid digitization in these regions, however, is quickly changing the landscape.

Despite the variations across regions, one element consistently holds true: the impact of credit on people's financial lives. Understanding how credit systems work is important for anyone looking to handle the financial world successfully.

Now that we have a grasp of the credit system, let's explore the connection of psychology and finance. The way we handle money, particularly credit, is rooted in our psychological makeup. Our financial decisions are not always rational; they are often influenced by cognitive biases, emotional triggers, and social pressures.

Consider the concept of instant gratification, which is a classic psychological principle in which the desire for immediate pleasure can overshadow our goals. This principle is at play when someone chooses to buy a luxury item on credit, knowing it will take months, or even years, to pay off. The immediate joy of owning the item outweighs the future burden of debt.

Another aspect is the fear of missing out (FOMO). Nowadays, seeing peers enjoy vacations, fancy dinners, and new gadgets can drive us to spend beyond our means, often relying on credit to keep up. This behavior is fueled by the need for social acceptance and the fear of being left out.

Moreover, financial stress and anxiety can significantly impact credit behavior. People under financial strain may make impulsive decisions, avoid dealing with their credit issues, or even engage in risky financial behaviors as a coping mechanism.

WHY THIS BOOK IS UNIQUE

Now, you might wonder, with so many personal finance books out there, what makes this one unique? The answer lies in its approach. Most financial advice focuses purely on the numbers—budgets, interest rates, investment returns—topics that, for most people, are hard to digest and understand. But, while these are undoubtedly important, they only tell part of the story.

This book goes beyond the numbers to explore the psychological principles that underpin our financial behavior. It's not just about how to manage money but why we manage it the way we do.

In the chapters that follow, you'll look into various aspects of credit and personal finance through a psychological lens. We'll start with the foundations of credit—how it works, why it matters, and what the different components are—and from there, we'll go into the psychological principles that influence our financial behavior, examining topics such as cognitive biases, emotional triggers, and social pressures.

You'll also be equipped with practical advice on managing credit and personal finance, including strategies for improving your credit score, managing debt, and many more.

Additionally, we'll address some of the common challenges people face when it comes to credit and personal finance, such as dealing with financial stress, overcoming bad financial habits, and facing major financial decisions.

Ultimately, this book is about more than just managing credit and finances—it's about creating a sense of financial well-being. If we understand the psychological principles behind our financial behavior, we can make better decisions, and achieve greater financial stability.

So, whether you're looking to improve your credit score, get out of debt, or simply gain a better understanding of your financial behavior, this book is here to guide you. Let's explore the connection between psychology and finance and discover new ways to take control of your financial future. Welcome to *The Credit Conundrum*.

CHAPTER I

THE HISTORICAL EVOLUTION OF CREDIT

C redit is not just a tool for economic transactions; it is a base of modern civilization that is connected with our psychological and social aspects—and for good reason. Understanding the historical context of credit is essential to know its impact on our lives today. Our current psychological associations with credit —trust, risk, opportunity, and obligation—are connected with its historical evolution.

That's why, in this chapter, we're going back in time, exploring the origins, transformations, and milestones of credit systems from ancient civilizations to the digital age. With this, we can better understand the psychological principles that underpin personal finance and credit management today.

THE ORIGINS OF CREDIT

The story of credit begins in the ancient world. Yes, in countries like Mesopotamia, Greece, and Egypt, credit existed, but not the way we know it today. At that time, early forms of credit emerged as essential tools for trade and commerce.

In ancient Mesopotamia, one of the cradles of civilization, the concept of credit was born out of necessity. Clay tablets dating back to 2100 B.C.E. reveal records of loans, where farmers would borrow seeds for planting and repay the debt after the harvest (Tyler, 1999). These transactions were based on trust and mutual benefit, laying the groundwork for more complex credit systems.

Ancient Egypt also had sophisticated credit practices. Temples and granaries acted as early banks, storing surplus grain and lending it out to farmers in need. These loans were meticulously recorded on papyrus scrolls, creating a written trail of credit transactions that ensured accountability (Ahmed, 2021).

In ancient Greece, the introduction of money lending marked a great advancement. Greek merchants and traders frequently engaged in credit transactions, using rudimentary contracts to formalize their agreements (Stevens Leese, 2014). This period saw the beginnings of interest charges, which compensated lenders for the risk of loaning their money.

Rome further refined these practices, with the *argentarii* (Roman bankers) having an important role in the economy. They provided loans to people and businesses, facilitating trade and commerce across the Roman Empire. The Roman legal system also recognized and enforced loan contracts, adding a layer of security to credit transactions (Jolowicz and Glendon, n.d.).

Barter Systems and the Introduction of Money Lending

Before the widespread use of money, barter systems were the primary means of trade. However, barter had its limitations, primarily the need for a double coincidence of wants or a direct exchange between two parties. The introduction of money—first as metal coins and later as paper currency—revolutionized trade by providing a common medium of exchange.

Money lending soon followed, allowing people and businesses to borrow currency for various purposes. In ancient civilizations, money lending was often informal and based on personal relationships. However, as societies grew, more formalized credit systems began to appear, with specific rules and regulations governing lending practices.

As you can see, credit was an important part of early trade and commerce, enabling merchants to conduct business over long distances and periods. For instance, a merchant in ancient Greece might borrow money to purchase goods from Egypt, sell those goods in Athens, and repay the loan from the proceeds. This system facilitated the flow of goods and services, contributing to economic growth and prosperity.

THE MIDDLE AGES AND RENAISSANCE

Now, let's move to the Middle Ages and the Renaissance. These were periods for credit, marked by the emergence of banking families, the prohibition of usury, and the development of bills of exchange.

During the medieval period, powerful banking families such as the Medicis in Florence and the Fuggers in Augsburg rose to prominence. These families established banks that provided a range of financial services, including loans, deposits, and currency exchange (Mwelwa, 2023). The Medici Bank, founded in the 14th century, pioneered innovative practices such as double-entry bookkeeping, which improved accuracy and transparency in financial transactions.

The Church's Stance on Usury and Its Impact on Credit Practices

The Catholic Church's prohibition of usury—charging interest on loans—posed significant challenges for medieval bankers. Usury was considered a sin, and those found guilty of it faced severe penalties. To handle this moral dilemma, bankers devised creative ways to charge interest without violating Church doctrine. For example, they might embed interest charges within the principal amount or label them as fees for services.

Despite these restrictions, the demand for credit continued to grow, and informal lending practices flourished. The Church's stance on usury also led to the development of alternative financial instruments, such as partnership agreements and profit-sharing arrangements.

The Development of Bills of Exchange and Their Role in International Trade

The Renaissance period saw the introduction of bills of exchange, which revolutionized international trade. These financial instruments allowed merchants to conduct business across long distances without the need to carry large amounts of physical currency.

A bill of exchange was essentially a written order to pay a specified amount of money at a future date. For example, a merchant in Venice could issue a bill of exchange to a trading partner in London, promising payment upon the delivery of goods. The recipient could then sell the bill to another party, creating a transferable credit instrument that facilitated trade.

THE BIRTH OF MODERN CREDIT SYSTEMS

The Renaissance also was the pioneer of modern credit systems, with the establishment of the first banks in Italy and the spread of banking practices to Northern Europe.

The First Banks in Renaissance Italy

Renaissance Italy was the birthplace of modern banking, with institutions such as the Medici Bank in Florence and the Banco di San Giorgio in Genoa setting new standards for financial services (Mwelwa, 2023). These banks offered a range of credit products, including loans, letters of credit, and bills of exchange, which facilitated trade and commerce.

The Spread of Banking to Northern Europe

The innovations pioneered in Italy soon spread to Northern Europe. In the Netherlands, the establishment of the Amsterdam Exchange Bank in 1609 marked a point in its history. This bank provided a stable currency exchange and deposit services, reducing the risk and complexity of international trade.

In England, the founding of the Bank of England in 1694 further advanced banking practices. As a central bank, it played a role in managing the national debt and issuing banknotes, which became widely accepted as a reliable medium of exchange. The British banking model influenced financial systems worldwide, setting the stage for modern central banking.

The 18th and 19th centuries saw the emergence of consumer credit, with merchants extending credit to customers for everyday purchases. Installment plans became popular, allowing consumers to buy goods on credit and pay for them over time. This development made high-value items such as furniture and appliances accessible to a broader segment of the population, fueling economic growth and consumerism.

CREDIT IN THE AGE OF INDUSTRIALIZATION

Around the turn of the 19th century, the Industrial Revolution marked a period of rapid economic transformation, driven by technological advancements and the expansion of credit.

The construction of factories, railways, and infrastructure projects required substantial capital investment. Entrepreneurs and industrialists turned to banks and investors for loans, often securing credit based on their projected profits. This practice not only spurred industrial growth but also democratized investment, allowing a broader swath of society to participate in economic expansion.

In this period, credit was important for financing industrial enterprises and urban development. Municipal bonds became a common tool for funding public works projects, such as roads, bridges, and public buildings. This era of rapid urbanization was underpinned by a robust credit system that supported large-scale infrastructure projects.

The Introduction of Credit Instruments Like Bonds and Stock Certificates

The Industrial Revolution also saw the introduction of new financial instruments such as bonds and stock certificates. These instruments allowed businesses and governments to raise capital by issuing debt or equity to investors.

The Construction of the Transcontinental Railroad

One of the most ambitious projects of the 19th century, the Transcontinental Railroad, exemplifies the critical role of credit in industrial expansion. The Union Pacific and Central Pacific railroads secured significant loans from banks and issued bonds to investors to finance the project (American Battlefield Trust, 2022). Despite immense financial and logistical challenges, the completion of the railroad in 1869 changed American commerce, linking the East and West coasts and opening up new markets for goods and services.

The Rise of the Steel Industry

Andrew Carnegie's steel empire is another great example. Carnegie used credit to build and expand his steel mills, securing loans from banks and reinvesting profits into technological advancements (Steele Gordon, n.d.). The availability of credit allowed Carnegie to innovate continuously, reducing production costs and eventually dominating the steel industry.

THE 20TH CENTURY AND THE AMERICAN INFLUENCE

To understand this era easily, let's do a little activity. Imagine that you're in the early 1920s, and America is filled with optimism. The economy is booming, and a new culture of consumerism is taking root. People are eager to enjoy the newfound prosperity, and credit becomes the key to unlocking their dreams.

Here, you'll meet Kate, a young schoolteacher in Chicago. She has her eye on a brand-new washing machine, a marvel of modern technology that promises to make her household chores much easier. The problem? She doesn't have money to buy it. But Kate's local department store offers a solution: installment credit, which means that she can take the washing machine home today and pay for it in small, manageable monthly payments.

This installment plan quickly becomes popular, allowing ordinary Americans to purchase big-ticket items like appliances, furniture, and even pianos. Stores across the country adopt this model, and consumer credit becomes a cornerstone of the American economy.

The 20th century brought about significant changes in credit practices, particularly in the US. The early 20th century saw a dramatic rise in consumer credit, driven by a booming economy and the proliferation of new credit products.

The introduction of auto loans and mortgages revolutionized the way Americans financed large purchases. Auto loans enabled consumers to buy cars and pay for them over time, while mortgages made homeownership accessible to a broader population. These credit products fueled economic growth and transformed the American landscape.

The advent of credit cards in the mid–20th century further expanded consumer credit. Companies like Diners Club, American Express, and Bank of America introduced credit cards that allowed consumers to make purchases and pay off their balances over time. Credit cards quickly became a ubiquitous part of daily life. At this time, people were happy with their credits, but nothing lasts forever.

The Great Depression and Its Impact

The Great Depression of the 1930s had a big impact on credit practices and regulations. The economic collapse revealed the dangers of unchecked credit expansion and speculation.

Regulatory Reforms

In response to the crisis, the government introduced significant regulatory reforms to restore confidence in the financial system. The Glass-Steagall Act of 1933 separated commercial and investment banking, reducing risk. The Federal Deposit Insurance Corporation (FDIC) was created to insure bank deposits, protecting consumers from bank failures (Heakal, 2024).

The Securities and Exchange Commission (SEC)

The SEC was established to oversee the stock market and curb speculative practices. These reforms stabilized the financial system and laid the groundwork for modern regulatory frameworks.

THE DEVELOPMENT OF CREDIT SCORING

The late 20th century saw the development of credit scoring systems, which changed the financial landscape by providing a standardized method to assess creditworthiness.

Credit bureaus such as Equifax, Experian, and TransUnion began compiling extensive databases of consumer credit information. These bureaus collected data on people's borrowing and repayment histories, creating credit reports that lenders could use to assess risk.

Creation of the FICO Score

In 1956, engineer William R. Fair and mathematician Earl J. Isaac founded Fair, Isaac and Company (FICO). They developed a statistical model to predict a borrower's likelihood of repaying a loan, resulting in the FICO score (Makhado, 2023). By the 1980s, major credit bureaus began incorporating FICO scores into their reports, and the FICO score quickly became the industry standard for credit evaluation.

The introduction of credit scores had effects on both consumers and lenders. For consumers, the transparency of credit-scoring systems encouraged responsible financial management. People began paying closer attention to their credit habits, understanding that timely payments and responsible borrowing would positively impact their scores.

For lenders, credit scoring provided a more efficient and objective way to assess risk. The use of FICO scores allowed banks and financial institutions to streamline their loan approval processes, making credit decisions faster and more accurate.

The Digital Revolution and Credit

The turn of the 21st century brought about a digital revolution that changed credit systems, introduced innovative financial technologies (fintech), and fundamentally altered how people access and perceive credit.

The advent of online banking and fintech innovations revolutionized finances. Consumers could now manage their finances from the comfort of their homes, reducing the need for in-person visits and paperwork. Fintech startups introduced new credit solutions, such as instant loans, digital wallets, and credit-monitoring apps, streamlining the credit application process.

Digital platforms also gave rise to peer-to-peer (P2P) lending and microfinance, providing alternative credit sources outside traditional banking systems. P2P lending platforms like LendingClub and Prosper connected borrowers directly with individual investors, offering competitive interest rates and flexible terms (Basha et al., 2021). Microfinance platforms like Kiva enabled people worldwide to lend small amounts to entrepreneurs in developing countries, empowering people to start businesses and achieve financial independence.

These platforms have democratized access to credit, breaking down barriers that once excluded many from the financial system. Mobile banking and digital wallets provided financial services to remote and underserved areas, ensuring more people could benefit from credit. Credit score transparency improved financial literacy, helping consumers understand and monitor their credit health.

SUMMARY

As you can see, each milestone in the history of credit has influenced public perception and the psychological relationship with credit, shaping societal norms and attitudes toward debt.

The origins of credit in ancient civilizations were based on trust and mutual benefit, instilling a sense of responsibility and reciprocity in financial transactions. The Middle Ages introduced ethical considerations with the Church's stance on usury, highlighting the moral implications of lending and borrowing.

The development of banking institutions and financial instruments during the Renaissance and Industrial Revolution built trust in credit systems. The establishment of credit bureaus and the introduction of credit scoring provided transparency and reliability, enhancing consumer confidence.

Finally, the rise of consumer credit in the 20th century democratized access to credit, making it an integral part of daily life. The digital revolution further expanded access, allowing people to manage their credit and financial health proactively.

Our journey through the history of credit, from ancient times to the present day, reveals the impact of credit on economic growth and personal finance. Understanding the historical evolution of credit helps us discover its psychological implications and societal influence.

As we move forward, we will look at the psychological principles that drive financial decision-making. In the next chapter, we will explore how cognitive biases, emotional triggers, and social influences shape our financial behaviors and attitudes.

CHAPTER 2

UNDERSTANDING THE FINANCIAL MINDSET

Your financial mindset determines your approach to money; it influences every financial decision you make, from daily spending habits to long-term financial planning. But what exactly is a financial mindset, and how does it develop? In this chapter, we'll explore the different types of financial mindsets—ranging from abundance to scarcity—and how they shape our financial behaviors. You'll also learn about the factors that influence your financial mindset, including early life experiences, cultural backgrounds, and personality traits.

But before we begin, think about your financial mindset and look at it as the lens through which you view the world of money. This lens colors your perceptions, guiding your actions and decisions. Some people view money through a lens of abundance, seeing endless possibilities and opportunities. Others may have a scarcity mindset, constantly worried about not having enough. These mindsets aren't just abstract ideas; they have real effects on your financial life and the decisions you make.

For example, someone with an abundance mindset might feel confident in making investments, believing that the potential rewards outweigh the risks. On the other hand, a person with a scarcity mindset might avoid investing altogether, paralyzed by the fear of loss. Understanding where you fall on this spectrum is the first step toward gaining control over your financial future.

TYPES OF FINANCIAL MINDSETS

The Abundance Mindset

People with an *abundance mindset* believe that there are enough resources and opportunities for everyone. They see money as a tool that can be used to create more wealth—not just for themselves but for others, as well. This mindset is often associated with optimism, generosity, and a willingness to take calculated risks.

Those with an abundance mindset tend to be more entrepreneurial, are open to new opportunities, and view financial setbacks as temporary obstacles rather than permanent failures. They are likely to invest in their education, businesses, and relationships, believing that these investments will yield returns in the long run. This mindset can lead to proactive financial behaviors, such as consistent saving, investing, and strategic planning. However, if not balanced, it might also lead to overconfidence and taking on too much risk.

The Scarcity Mindset

In contrast, the *scarcity mindset* is rooted in the belief that resources are limited and must be hoarded or protected. People with this mindset often focus on what they lack rather than what they have, leading to fear-based financial decisions.

Those who think in terms of scarcity often hesitate to accept financial opportunities, even when the potential benefits greatly exceed the associated risks. They might be overly frugal, resist spending on necessary items, or miss out on opportunities because they fear losing what little they have. This mindset can lead to overly conservative financial behaviors, such as avoiding investments or refusing to spend on education or personal growth. While this mindset might protect against loss in the short term, it can also limit long-term financial growth and opportunities.

The Fixed Mindset vs. the Growth Mindset

In addition to abundance and scarcity mindsets, your financial mindset can also be categorized as fixed or growth-oriented.

- **Fixed mindset:** People with a fixed mindset believe that their financial situation is static and unchangeable. They may feel resigned to their current circumstances, thinking that they will never be able to improve their financial situation, leading to inaction as people may feel that any effort to change their situation is futile.
- **Growth mindset:** Conversely, those with a growth mindset believe that they can improve their financial situation through effort and learning. They are more likely to seek out new opportunities, invest in their personal development, and take proactive steps to achieve their financial goals.

SHAPING YOUR FINANCIAL MINDSET

Your financial mindset doesn't develop in a vacuum; it is shaped by a series of factors, including your early life experiences, cultural background, and inherent personality traits.

Early Life Experiences

Starting with early life experiences, the financial lessons you learned as a child often have an impact on your financial mindset. If you grew up in a household where money was tight, you might have developed a scarcity mindset, constantly worried about not having enough. On the other hand, if your family was financially stable and had open discussions about money, you might have developed a more positive and proactive approach to financial management.

Cultural Background

Cultural attitudes and values significantly influence financial behavior. Various cultures exhibit distinct perspectives on money management, savings, expenditures, and debt, which can shape how people approach their finances.

In collectivist cultures, there may be a greater emphasis on communal wealth and shared financial responsibilities. People from these cultures tend to prioritize family and community needs over individual financial goals. In contrast, individualist cultures often emphasize personal financial independence and the pursuit of individual wealth.

Also, cultural attitudes toward debt can vary. In some cultures, taking on debt is seen as a normal part of life, necessary for achieving important goals such as buying a home or starting a business. In others, debt is viewed with suspicion and is avoided whenever possible.

Personality Traits

Your personality traits also influence your financial mindset. Some people are naturally more risk-averse, while others are more willing to take financial risks. Understanding your personality can help you identify potential strengths and weaknesses in your financial mindset.

- **Risk tolerance:** People with high risk tolerance are more likely to pursue investment opportunities, while those with low risk tolerance often prefer safer options like savings accounts or bonds.
- **Impulsivity:** Impulsive people may struggle with saving and budgeting, often making spontaneous purchases without considering the long-term consequences.
- **Future orientation:** People who are more future-oriented are likely to prioritize long-term financial planning and saving for retirement, while those who are more present-focused might prioritize immediate gratification.

CREDIT BASICS

Now that we've explored how your financial mindset is shaped, let's look at the real reason why this book is written: credit. Understanding the basics of credit is very important for facing our finances effectively.

Credit is the backbone of modern finance, impacting everything from individual purchasing power to the broader economy. At its core, credit is the ability to borrow money or access goods or services with the understanding that you will repay the debt later (Investopedia, 2024). However, the way credit is assessed, reported, and managed varies across different systems and countries.

Credit Scores: A Broader View

Credit-scoring systems are used worldwide to assess the credit-worthiness of people and businesses. While the fundamental principle is similar—evaluating the likelihood of a borrower repaying their debt—the specific methods and scoring models can vary significantly across different countries and regions. Here are some of them, according to Capital One (2023):

Credit Scoring Systems Around the World

- **United States**

  - **FICO score:** The most widely used credit score in the US, ranging from 300 to 850. It evaluates elements such as payment history, total debts, duration of credit experience, recent credit inquiries, and categories of credit utilized.
  - **VantageScore:** Another major scoring model created by the three major credit bureaus (Equifax, Experian, and TransUnion). It also ranges from 300 to 850 and uses similar factors to the FICO score.

- **United Kingdom**

  - ○ **Experian, Equifax, and TransUnion:** These credit-reference agencies provide scores that typically range from 0 to 999 (Experian), 0 to 700 (Equifax), and 0 to 710 (TransUnion).

- **Canada**

  - ○ **Equifax and TransUnion:** The primary credit bureaus in Canada, with scores ranging from 300 to 900

- **European Union**

  - ○ **Schufa (Germany):** A credit-rating agency that provides scores ranging from 0 to 1,000, with higher scores indicating lower risk
  - ○ **Creditreform (Austria):** Offers a credit scoring model similar to Schufa

- **Japan**

  - ○ **CIC (Credit Information Center):** Provides a credit-scoring system used by most lenders in Japan

- **Australia**

  - ○ **Equifax, Experian, and illion:** The major credit-reporting agencies in Australia, with scores typically ranging from 0 to 1,200

- **China**

  - **Sesame Credit (Zhima Credit):** A popular credit-scoring system run by Ant Financial, ranging from 350 to 950
  - **People's Bank of China (PBOC):** The official credit-scoring system used by the central bank

- **India**

  - **CIBIL Score:** Provided by TransUnion CIBIL, with scores ranging from 300 to 900
  - **Experian, Equifax, and CRIF High Mark:** Other credit bureaus providing similar score ranges

- **Brazil**

  - **Boa Vista and Serasa Experian:** The main credit bureaus, with scores typically ranging from 0 to 1,000

- **South Africa**

  - **Compuscan, TransUnion, and Experian:** The primary credit bureaus, with scores ranging from 300 to 850

Common Factors in Credit Scores

Despite the differences in scoring models and ranges, there are common factors that influence credit scores across different systems:

- **Payment history:** Whether a person has paid past credit accounts on time
- **Amounts owed:** The total amount of debt a person has and the utilization rate of available credit
- **Length of credit history:** The duration of time a client has been using credit
- **Types of credit used:** The mix of credit accounts, such as credit cards, mortgages, and auto loans
- **New credit:** The number of recently opened credit accounts and inquiries

These scoring systems can help people better manage their credit profiles globally.

Credit Reports

A credit report provides a detailed history of a person's credit activities, including information on credit accounts, payment history, outstanding debts, and recent inquiries. Credit bureaus maintain credit reports, and they serve as the basis for calculating credit scores. Regularly checking your credit report is essential to ensure its accuracy and to identify potential issues, such as identity theft or errors.

Credit Bureaus

What exactly are credit bureaus? These are organizations that collect and maintain individual credit information. They provide credit reports to lenders, employers, and other authorized parties. But it's important to be aware that credit bureaus operate differently depending on the country, as shown here:

Credit Bureaus Overview

- **Equifax:** It operates globally and strongly focuses on data analytics and detailed credit histories. Present in the US, UK, Canada, Australia, India, and South Africa.
- **Experian:** Known for using alternative data in credit scoring and providing both FICO and its own Experian PLUS Score. Operates in more than 40 countries.
- **TransUnion:** Focuses on consumer credit monitoring with a proprietary VantageScore. Present in the US, UK, Canada, India, and South Africa.

Country-Specific Differences

- **US and UK:** All three bureaus dominate, but credit scores can vary slightly due to different algorithms.
- **Australia, Canada, India, South Africa:** Equifax and TransUnion share the market with local bureaus, offering region-specific credit reporting.

Each bureau will have slightly different information, so it's crucial to review reports from all three regularly. Understanding these basic components will take you to effective credit management.

As you can see, understanding your financial mindset is important in the world of personal finance and credit management. If you recognize the factors that shape your financial mindset—early life experiences, cultural background, and personality traits—you can gain insight into your financial behaviors and make more informed decisions.

CHAPTER 3

THE CREDIT SCORE AND FINANCIAL IDENTITY

Your credit score, a simple number ranging from 300 to 850 in most systems, holds a lot of power. It can determine whether you're approved for a loan, the interest rate you'll pay, and even your eligibility for certain jobs. But beyond its practical implications, the credit score plays a role in shaping your financial identity and influencing your behaviors. In this chapter, you'll go into the construction of financial identity through credit scores, the stigma associated with poor credit, and the psychological strategies for improving credit scores.

THE CONSTRUCTION OF FINANCIAL IDENTITY THROUGH CREDIT SCORES

A credit score is calculated based on factors such as payment history, amounts owed, length of credit history, types of credit used, and new credit inquiries. But, while it's a tool for lenders to assess risk, it's also much more than that—it's a reflection of your financial identity. But what does that mean? What is financial identity, anyway?

Your financial identity is the image you hold of yourself in the context of money management. It encompasses how you view your financial habits, your relationship with debt, and your confidence in making financial decisions. For many, the credit score is a central component of this identity. It's a number that can evoke feelings of pride, shame, anxiety, or satisfaction, depending on where you fall on the scale.

Consider this: When you check your credit score, what thoughts and emotions come to mind? Do you feel in control and confident, or do you experience stress and worry? These reactions indicate how your credit score is tied to your financial identity.

The Role of Credit Scores in Self-Perception

Credit scores influence how people perceive their financial competence. A high credit score is often seen as a badge of honor —a sign of responsibility, reliability, and success. It can boost self-esteem and reinforce positive financial behaviors. On the other hand, a low credit score can have the opposite effect, leading to feelings of inadequacy, shame, and anxiety.

Societal norms and expectations reinforce this connection between credit scores and self-perception. In a culture where financial success is often equated with personal success, a low credit score can feel like a mark of failure, leading to a negative feedback loop where people with poor credit scores become discouraged, making it harder for them to take the necessary steps to improve their financial situation.

The Social Comparison Trap

Another psychological aspect of credit scores is the tendency to engage in social comparison. Just as people compare their physical appearance, job status, or social lives to others, they also compare their credit scores. This can be particularly challenging in social settings where financial success is openly discussed, such as within certain professional circles or among friends and family.

For example, suppose you discover that your peers have higher credit scores. In that case, you might feel a sense of inadequacy or pressure to "catch up," which can lead to stress and even risky financial behaviors, such as taking on more debt in an attempt to boost your score quickly. Understanding the psychological impact of social comparison is crucial for maintaining a healthy relationship with your credit score and financial identity.

THE STIGMA ASSOCIATED WITH POOR CREDIT

While a good credit score can enhance your financial identity, a poor credit score often carries a significant stigma. This stigma can affect not only how others perceive you but also how you perceive yourself.

The Psychological Burden of Poor Credit

For many, having a low credit score feels like carrying a heavy burden. It's a constant reminder of past financial mistakes or challenges, whether due to overspending, unexpected medical bills, or job loss. The psychological burden can manifest in various ways:

- **Shame and embarrassment:** People with poor credit scores often feel ashamed of their financial situation. This shame can be exacerbated by the fear of being judged by others, whether it's a lender, an employer, or even a potential romantic partner.
- **Anxiety and stress:** The uncertainty of being approved for loans or the fear of facing higher interest rates can lead to ongoing anxiety. This stress can affect other areas of life, including personal relationships and mental health.
- **Avoidance behavior:** Some people with poor credit scores may engage in avoidance behavior, such as ignoring bills, avoiding credit applications, or refusing to discuss their financial situation. While this might provide temporary relief, it often leads to further financial difficulties and a worsening credit score.

The stigma associated with poor credit can also have tangible consequences on opportunities. In many cases, credit scores are used not only for loan approvals but also for job applications, rental agreements, and insurance rates. This means that a low credit score can limit access to better job opportunities, housing, and even financial products designed to help improve credit.

Employers often evaluate credit histories during the hiring process, especially for roles that carry financial obligations. A poor credit score might be seen as a red flag, which can be particularly frustrating for people who are otherwise qualified for the job but are held back by their credit history.

STRATEGIES FOR IMPROVING CREDIT SCORES

Building Financial Confidence

One of the first steps in improving a credit score is building financial confidence—you need to try shifting your mindset from one of fear and avoidance to one of empowerment and control. Here's how you can start:

- **Education:** Knowledge is power. If you educate yourself about how credit scores are calculated and what factors influence them, you can demystify the process and take informed actions. Understanding that every small positive action—such as making a payment on time or reducing your credit card balance—can contribute to improving your score can help you build confidence.
- **Setting achievable goals:** Start by setting small, achievable financial goals. For example, focus on paying down one credit card or consistently paying bills on time for three months. These small victories can build momentum and boost your confidence.
- **Mindset shifts:** Practice reframing your thoughts about money and credit. Instead of viewing your credit score as a fixed measure of your financial worth, see it as a dynamic number that you have the power to improve. This shift in perspective can reduce feelings of helplessness and encourage proactive financial behavior.

Practical Steps to Improve Your Credit Score

Improving a credit score requires a combination of strategic actions and consistent financial habits.

Pay Bills on Time

Consistently paying your bills on time is one of the most effective ways to improve your score. Consider setting up automatic payments or reminders to ensure you don't miss any due dates.

Reducing Balances

Maintaining high balances on your credit cards compared to your total credit limit can adversely affect your credit score. Aim to pay down your balances to below 30% of your credit limit, and if possible, pay them off in full each month.

Limit New Credit Applications

Each time you seek credit, a hard inquiry appears on your credit report, which can temporarily decrease your score. Choose your applications wisely and refrain from opening several accounts within a brief timeframe.

Check Your Credit Report Regularly

Regularly reviewing your credit report can help you identify and correct errors that may be negatively affecting your score. You have the right to receive a complimentary credit report from each of the three primary credit bureaus once per year. Take advantage of this to ensure your report is accurate.

Consider a Secured Credit Card

Consider applying for a secured credit card to enhance your chances of getting a traditional credit card despite a low credit score. This type of card requires a deposit that establishes your credit limit. If you use the card wisely and consistently make timely payments, you can gradually improve your credit score.

THE PSYCHOLOGICAL REWARDS OF IMPROVING YOUR CREDIT SCORE

Watching your credit score improve can boost your confidence and reinforce positive financial behaviors. Each improvement is a tangible result of your efforts, validating the hard work you've put into managing your finances.

Also, a higher credit score often means better access to financial products, lower interest rates, and more favorable loan terms, which can reduce financial stress and provide a greater sense of security and stability.

Ultimately, as your credit score improves, so does your financial identity. You may find yourself feeling more in control of your financial future, which can lead to a more positive and empowered self-image.

As you can see, the credit score is much more than just a number; it's a powerful element of your financial identity, influencing how you view yourself and how others perceive you. While a high credit score can boost confidence and open doors, a low score can carry a heavy stigma, leading to feelings of shame, anxiety, and limited opportunities.

CHAPTER 4
SAVING
A PSYCHOLOGICAL PERSPECTIVE

S aving money might seem like a straightforward task—set aside a portion of your income regularly, and over time, you'll accumulate a tidy sum. Yet, for many people, the act of saving is fraught with challenges—not because of a lack of understanding or tools, but because of the psychological barriers that stand in the way. In this chapter, we'll explore these psychological obstacles, such as the allure of instant gratification and the struggle with self-control, and we'll provide strategies to help you cultivate a saver's mindset. By the end, you'll be equipped not only with practical tips but also with a deeper understanding of the mental shifts needed to build a robust financial cushion.

THE PSYCHOLOGICAL BARRIERS TO SAVING

To understand why saving can be so difficult, we need to look beyond the numbers and examine the psychological factors at play. These barriers are rooted in human behavior and can significantly influence our financial decisions.

Instant Gratification

At the heart of many saving struggles is the concept of instant grat-ification—the desire for immediate pleasure or satisfaction, often at the expense of long-term benefits. Imagine you're out shopping and see a new gadget that you've wanted for weeks. It's on sale, and buying it now feels like the perfect way to boost your mood. At that moment, the long-term goal of saving for something more substantial—like a vacation or a down payment on a house—fades into the background.

This scenario is a classic example of how instant gratification can derail saving efforts. Our brains are wired to prioritize immediate rewards over future gains, a concept known as *temporal discounting*. The further away a reward is in time, the less value we place on it. This psychological quirk can make it challenging to resist the temptation to spend now rather than save for later.

Lack of Self-Control

Self-control refers to the capacity to manage one's emotions, thoughts, and actions, particularly when faced with many tempta-tions. When it comes to saving money, self-control is crucial for resisting the urge to spend on nonessential items or experiences.

However, self-control isn't infinite. It can be depleted by stress, fatigue, and other demands on our mental resources. For example, after a long day at work, you might find it harder to resist ordering takeout instead of cooking at home, even though it's more expen-sive. This depletion of self-control can lead to impulsive spending, which makes saving money more difficult.

Our environment also plays a role in our ability to exercise self-control. We live in a world where we're constantly bombarded with advertisements, discounts, and social media posts showcasing other people's purchases. This constant exposure to spending opportunities can erode our self-control and make it more challenging to stick to saving goals.

Social Pressure and Comparison

Social pressure is another psychological barrier to saving. This pressure often stems from the desire to keep up with others, whether it's friends, family, or colleagues. The phenomenon often referred to as "keeping up with the Joneses" involves comparing oneself to others and feeling pressured to match their spending habits (CommonLit, 2014).

For instance, if your peers frequently dine at expensive restaurants, take luxurious vacations, or buy the latest tech gadgets, you might feel compelled to do the same, even if it means dipping into your savings or going into debt. The fear of missing out (FOMO) can drive you to prioritize short-term social satisfaction over long-term financial security.

Social media exacerbates this issue by creating a constant stream of curated, often idealized versions of other people's lives. It can create an unrealistic standard of living that fuels the desire to spend rather than save. Overcoming this pressure requires a strong sense of self-awareness and a commitment to your financial goals, independent of others' expectations.

CREATING A SAVER'S MINDSET

Understanding the psychological barriers to saving is the first step; the next is creating a mindset that supports consistent saving habits. Developing a saver's mindset involves shifting your perspective on money, setting clear goals, and creating habits that make saving a natural part of your financial routine.

Setting Clear Goals

Having clear, specific goals is crucial for motivating yourself to save. Instead of saving for a vague "future," set concrete goals with defined timelines. For example, you might set a goal to save $10,000 for an emergency fund within the next year or to contribute $500 per month to your retirement account.

Breaking goals into smaller, actionable steps can transform them into tangible achievements. For instance, if your goal is to save $10,000 in a year, that's about $833 per month, or roughly $28 per day. If you focus on these smaller increments, the goal becomes less daunting, and you're more likely to stay committed.

Regularly reassessing and modifying your objectives is crucial for sustained progress. Life circumstances can change, and your goals should be flexible enough to accommodate these changes. If you stay engaged with your goals, you can maintain a sense of purpose and direction in your saving efforts.

Automating Your Savings

Automating the process is one of the most effective ways to overcome psychological barriers to saving. Automation removes the need for willpower and reduces the temptation to spend money before it's saved.

Set up automatic transfers from your checking account to your savings account on a regular basis, such as monthly or biweekly. Treat these transfers as non-negotiable, similar to paying a bill. This way, you prioritize saving and ensure that it happens consistently, regardless of other spending temptations.

Automation can also be applied to retirement savings. If your employer offers a 401(k) or similar retirement plan, enroll in automatic contributions directly from your paycheck. This strategy not only helps you save regularly but also takes advantage of compound interest, which can significantly boost your savings over time.

Reframing Your Mindset Around Money

Reframing your mindset involves changing the way you think about saving and spending. Instead of viewing saving as a sacrifice or deprivation, reframe it as an investment in your future and a way to achieve financial freedom.

One technique for reframing is to focus on the value and security that saving provides rather than what you're giving up. For example, instead of thinking, *I can't afford to go out to dinner because I'm saving money*, think, *I'm choosing to save money so I can build a financial cushion that will protect me in case of an emergency*. This shift in perspective can make saving feel more empowering and less restrictive.

Another way to reframe your mindset is to create positive associations with saving. Celebrate your saving milestones, no matter how small. Whether it's reaching a certain amount in your savings account or consistently saving for a few months, acknowledge your progress and reward yourself with a small treat or experience that aligns with your financial goals.

BUILDING A ROBUST FINANCIAL CUSHION

With the right mindset and strategies in place, you can begin to build a solid financial cushion—an essential component of financial security. A financial cushion provides you with the peace of mind and flexibility to handle unexpected expenses, pursue opportunities, and achieve your long-term financial goals.

The Importance of an Emergency Fund

An emergency fund is the foundation of financial security. It represents a reserve of money set aside specifically to cover unexpected expenses, such as medical bills, car repairs, or sudden job loss. This fund allows you to face life's uncertainties without the added stress of financial strain. Financial expert Elizabeth Gravier (2024) recommends that people aim to save three to six months' worth of living expenses in an easily accessible account, such as a high-yield savings account. This recommendation is based on the understanding that such a cushion can prevent financial disasters.

Having an emergency fund is not just about money; it offers you peace of mind. It reduces the anxiety associated with potential financial crises and provides the assurance that you won't need to resort to high-interest debt, such as credit cards, to cover emergencies. There are many psychological benefits to having an emergency fund. It changes your approach to financial management, shifting your focus from merely surviving from paycheck to paycheck to proactively managing your financial well-being.

The Psychological Impact of an Emergency Fund

The presence of an emergency fund can have a great psychological impact. The very act of saving money for future uncertainties can lead to a greater sense of control over your life. This control reduces the stress and anxiety that often accompany financial instability. When you have an emergency fund, you're financially prepared as well as emotionally and mentally prepared to handle unexpected challenges.

The connection between financial stability and mental well-being is well-documented. If you create and maintain an emergency fund, you're taking a proactive step to protect not just your finances but your mental health, as well.

Building an Emergency Fund: Strategies and Tips

Building an emergency fund requires discipline, commitment, and a strategic approach. It's not something that happens overnight, but with consistent effort, you can establish a substantial financial safety net. Here are some strategies to create one:

Start Small and Build Gradually

If the idea of saving three to six months' worth of expenses feels overwhelming, start with a smaller goal. For instance, aim to save $1,000 initially. This smaller goal can serve as a psychological boost, giving you a sense of accomplishment and motivation to continue saving. Once you reach this initial milestone, you can gradually increase your savings target, working toward the recommended three to six months' worth of living expenses.

Starting small also helps you develop the habit of saving. Saving money is like building a muscle—the more you practice, the stronger it becomes. By setting small, achievable goals, you're training yourself to prioritize saving and make it a regular part of your financial routine.

Prioritize Saving Over Spending

Treat your emergency fund as a top financial priority—allocate a portion of your income to your emergency fund before spending on nonessential items. This approach, often referred to as "paying yourself first," ensures that your savings grow consistently over time.

Keep Your Emergency Fund Separate

You'll want to keep your emergency fund in a separate account from your regular checking or spending accounts. Doing so reduces the temptation to dip into the fund for non-emergencies. When your emergency fund is out of sight, you're less likely to view it as an extension of your regular spending money.

A high-yield savings account serves as an excellent option for your emergency fund. It ensures quick access to your funds, when necessary, while also creating a barrier that discourages spending it on regular expenses. Additionally, a high-yield savings account allows your money to earn interest, helping your emergency fund grow over time.

Choosing a high-yield savings account is crucial. Certain banks and credit unions present more attractive interest rates and lower fees compared with their competitors. It's wise to shop around and compare options to find the best one that fits your needs. You might also consider factors like online access and customer service when making your decision. A good account should not only keep your money safe but also provide easy ways to transfer funds in case of an emergency. Finding a platform that feels comfortable and secure can provide peace of mind as you focus on building your savings.

Replenish Your Fund After Use

If you need to dip into your emergency fund, make it a priority to replenish it as soon as possible. The whole point of an emergency fund is to have it available when you need it, so if you've used part of it, it's important to restore it to its full amount, ensuring that it remains intact for future needs.

Replenishing your emergency fund should be treated with the same urgency as building it in the first place. If you've had to use your fund, re-evaluate your budget to find areas where you can cut back temporarily until your emergency fund is back to its original level. Replenishing your fund helps ensure that you're always prepared for the unexpected without having to rely on credit or other forms of debt.

The Link Between Saving and Psychology

Saving money is connected to our psychology. From battling the lure of instant gratification to creating a saver's mindset, it's clear that our financial behaviors are shaped by much more than just numbers on a spreadsheet. When you save money, you're setting aside cash while making a statement about your priorities and your willingness to delay gratification for long-term security.

Creating a saver's mindset involves changing the way you think about money. It's about viewing saving as a positive, empowering act rather than a sacrifice. This shift in mindset can have an impact on your financial behavior. Instead of feeling deprived when you save, you'll begin to feel a sense of pride and accomplishment, making it easier to continue saving and to build an even larger financial cushion.

But saving is just one piece of the puzzle. To fully understand how we interact with money—whether it's saving, spending, investing, or managing debt—we need to go even deeper into the psychological foundations of financial behavior. In the next chapter, you'll take a look at the emotional triggers and social influences that drive our financial decisions. With these points, you'll gain insights into how to make more informed and intentional financial choices.

CHAPTER 5

THE PSYCHOLOGICAL FOUNDATIONS OF FINANCIAL BEHAVIOR

M anaging credit effectively is not just a matter of understanding interest rates and payment schedules; you also need to understand the psychology that shapes our financial decisions. Why do we sometimes make choices that seem to go against our best financial interests? To answer this question, we must go into the psychological foundations of financial behavior. Behavioral economics, a field that merges insights from psychology and economics, offers a powerful lens through which we can examine the often irrational ways in which we handle credit and debt—so, let's jump in and learn about it.

BEHAVIORAL ECONOMICS AND CREDIT USAGE

Traditional economic theory assumes that people are rational actors who make decisions that maximize their utility. Behavioral economics contests the conventional view by recognizing that our choices are frequently shaped by cognitive biases, emotions, and social influences, all of which can lead to illogical results. Nowhere is this more evident than with credit usage.

The Paradox of Credit Card Rewards and Overspending

Credit card rewards programs are designed to incentivize spending by offering points, cash back, or other perks for every dollar spent. On the surface, these rewards seem like a savvy financial move—after all, who wouldn't want to earn rewards for purchases they would make anyway? However, behavioral economics reveals a paradox: The very rewards designed to encourage smart spending can also lead to overspending.

The psychological principle of loss aversion plays a significant role here. *Loss aversion* refers to the tendency for people to prefer avoiding losses over acquiring equivalent gains. In the context of credit card rewards, consumers may feel that not using their credit card means losing out on potential rewards, driving them to spend more than they otherwise would. This behavior is further exacerbated by the mental accounting process, where people categorize money into different "accounts" (e.g., rewards points versus actual cash) and may treat rewards as "free money," leading to less cautious spending.

As a result, what begins as a strategy to maximize benefits can spiral into a pattern of increased spending and, ultimately, greater debt accumulation. The allure of rewards can overshadow the long-term consequences of carrying a credit card balance, which often comes with high interest rates that negate the value of the rewards earned. Instead, consider opting for a low-interest credit card or a card with a strong balance-transfer offer if you carry a balance. This approach helps minimize interest costs and encourages more responsible financial behavior, ensuring that the primary focus remains on maintaining financial health rather than chasing rewards.

The Impact of Present Bias on Credit Repayment Plans

Present bias is another key concept in behavioral economics that influences credit behavior. This bias highlights the inclination to favor short-term gains at the expense of greater long-term advantages, even when the latter are more substantial. In the context of credit management, present bias can lead to procrastination in paying off debt and a preference for making minimum payments rather than larger payments that would reduce the balance more quickly.

For example, when faced with a credit card bill, a person might choose to pay the minimum amount due because it allows them to retain more cash for immediate use. The immediate benefit of having extra cash on hand is given more weight than the long-term benefit of paying more than the minimum amount due, thereby reducing debt and avoiding interest charges. This behavior can trap people in a cycle of debt, where the balance grows faster than it can be paid off, leading to mounting interest charges and financial stress.

Present bias also manifests in the common practice of taking on new debt while still carrying existing debt. The temptation to make a new purchase or finance an expensive item on credit often overshadows the goal of paying down current debts, leading to a snowball effect of accumulating liabilities.

Mental Accounting and Its Effects on Debt Management

Mental accounting refers to the tendency of people to categorize their finances based on the money's origin or purpose, which can result in illogical financial choices. For example, someone might treat a tax refund or bonus as "extra" money and spend it frivolously, even though it could have been used to pay down existing debt.

In the context of credit management, mental accounting can lead to ineffective debt-repayment strategies. For example, a person might focus on paying off small debts first because it feels more manageable and provides a psychological win, even if it makes more financial sense to pay off the debt with the highest interest rate. This approach, often called the *snowball method*, is driven more by emotional satisfaction than by a rational assessment of what would minimize costs in the long run.

Mental accounting also influences how people perceive credit versus cash. Many people are more willing to spend on credit because it feels less tangible than spending cash. This detachment from the "real" money can lead to higher spending and, subsequently, higher debt.

COGNITIVE PROCESSES IN FINANCIAL DECISION-MAKING

Financial decisions involve complex cognitive processes, including perception, attention, memory, and reasoning. These processes can help explain why people might overestimate their ability to manage credit or underestimate the impact of debt.

Perception and Attention in Credit Usage

Perception plays a role in how people interpret and respond to financial information. For example, the way a credit offer is framed—whether it emphasizes the ease of obtaining credit or the potential risks—can significantly influence a person's decision to apply for and use credit. Similarly, attention, or the lack thereof, can lead to poor financial choices. Many people tend to overlook or downplay the importance of fine print in credit agreements, such as interest rates and fees, focusing instead on the immediate benefits.

Marketers often exploit these cognitive tendencies by highlighting the positive aspects of credit offers, such as low introductory rates or flexible payment options, while minimizing the long-term costs. As a result, consumers often find themselves in financial trouble because they fail to fully grasp the implications of the credit terms.

Memory and Reasoning in Debt Management

Our ability to recall past financial experiences, both positive and negative, can influence current and future decisions. For instance, someone who has previously experienced the stress of high credit card debt may be more cautious about taking on new debt. However, memory can be unreliable, especially when it comes to recalling complex financial information or calculating the long-term impact of debt. To counter this, it's helpful to keep a financial journal or regularly review your financial statements. If you document your experiences and decisions, you can create a clear, accurate record that guides future choices, ensuring that you base your financial decisions on solid data rather than relying solely on memory.

Reasoning, the cognitive process of evaluating information and making decisions, is essential for effective credit management. However, reasoning can be clouded by cognitive biases, such as overconfidence, where people believe they can manage their debt better than they actually can. This overconfidence can lead to risky financial behavior, such as taking on more debt than is manageable or underestimating the time and effort required to pay it off.

EMOTIONAL INFLUENCES ON FINANCIAL BEHAVIOR

Emotions can drive decisions that are not always in line with rational thinking, leading to behaviors that can either support or undermine financial well-being.

Overconfidence and Positive Emotions

Positive emotions, such as happiness, excitement, or optimism, can lead to overconfidence in financial decision-making. When people feel good, they may underestimate risks and overestimate their ability to manage financial challenges, resulting in taking on more debt, investing in risky ventures, or making large purchases on credit without fully considering the consequences.

For example, during periods of economic growth, when stock markets are booming and employment is high, people may feel more secure in their financial situation and take on additional credit to finance lifestyle upgrades. The optimism of the moment can overshadow the potential risks of an economic downturn or a personal financial setback.

Stress, Anxiety, and Impulsive Spending

These emotions can trigger impulsive spending as a coping mechanism, where people make purchases to alleviate emotional distress. This type of spending, often referred to as "retail therapy," can provide temporary relief but ultimately leads to financial regret and increased debt.

Stress and anxiety can also lead to avoidance behavior, where people ignore their financial situation, delay paying bills, or avoid addressing debt. This avoidance can exacerbate financial problems, leading to a cycle of increasing debt and worsening emotional distress.

Understanding the emotional influences on financial behavior is crucial for developing healthier credit habits. By recognizing how emotions drive financial decisions, people can learn to manage their emotional responses and make more rational, informed choices.

So, as you can see, the intersection of psychology and finance reveals that cognitive biases, emotional influences, and social pressures often shape our financial decisions. Behavioral economics provides valuable insights into why we sometimes make irrational decisions, particularly when it comes to managing credit and debt. Concepts such as loss aversion, present bias, and mental accounting help explain the paradoxes of credit card rewards, the challenges of debt repayment, and the pitfalls of financial decision-making.

Cognitive processes such as perception, memory, and reasoning, along with emotional influences such as overconfidence and stress, play a significant role in our financial behavior.

In the next chapter, you'll learn how these biases, such as overconfidence, confirmation bias, and anchoring, can lead to suboptimal financial decisions and how to develop strategies to overcome these challenges.

CHAPTER 6

COGNITIVE BIASES AND THEIR IMPACT ON CREDIT BEHAVIOR

When it comes to managing our finances, we like to think that we make decisions based on logic and careful consideration. However, the truth is that our financial decisions are often influenced by systematic patterns of deviation from rational judgment. These biases can lead us astray, causing us to make illogical decisions that may seem reasonable at the moment but can have detrimental long-term effects, especially when it comes to credit management.

In this chapter, we will explore some of the most common cognitive biases that impact credit behavior, such as overconfidence bias, optimism bias, anchoring, and the availability heuristic. Understanding these will not only help us recognize when they are influencing our financial behavior but also enable us to develop strategies to counteract them and make more rational credit decisions.

OVERCONFIDENCE BIAS

Overconfidence bias refers to the tendency to overestimate our abilities, including our ability to manage credit effectively, leading us to believe that we are more capable of handling financial challenges than we actually are, which can result in taking on more debt than we can realistically manage.

The Trap of Overestimating Our Financial Abilities

Imagine that you've been successfully managing one credit card for years, always paying off the balance in full each month. Encouraged by this success, you decide to open a second credit card, thinking that you'll be able to handle it just as well. After all, you've done it before, so why not again?

However, with the second card, your expenses increase—perhaps you're using it for a new set of purchases, or maybe the temptation to spend has grown with the added credit limit. Before long, you find yourself carrying a balance on both cards. But here's the catch: You still believe you can manage it, even as the interest starts to accumulate. You're confident that next month you'll pay it off, but next month comes, and the balance hasn't budged. This is overconfidence bias in action.

The Real Cost of Overconfidence

Overconfidence bias can lead to a dangerous cycle of debt. When we overestimate our ability to repay, we might miss payments or underestimate the impact of high interest rates. The cumulative burden of multiple credit card payments, especially when carrying balances across several cards, can quickly become overwhelming. The interest compounds, and what seemed manageable at first becomes a financial quagmire.

For instance, let's say you're carrying a $5,000 balance across two credit cards with an average interest rate of 20%. Even if you make the minimum payments, it could take years to pay off the debt, with a significant portion of your payments going toward interest rather than the principal. The overconfidence that led you to believe you could handle more debt than you actually could has now placed you in a position where it's challenging to regain control.

OPTIMISM BIAS

Optimism bias is the tendency to believe that we are less likely to experience negative events than others. While a positive outlook can be beneficial in many aspects of life, it can be detrimental when it comes to managing credit. This bias can lead us to underestimate the likelihood of financial setbacks, such as job loss, medical emergencies, or unexpected expenses, and consequently, we might over-rely on credit.

The Illusion of Financial Security

Consider someone who assumes that they will always have a steady income because they've never experienced a period of unemployment. This belief leads them to maintain minimal emergency savings while relying heavily on credit for discretionary spending. They might think, *I'll always be able to pay off my credit card next month because my paycheck will cover it*, but life is unpredictable, and financial setbacks can happen to anyone.

When a setback does occur—say, an unexpected medical bill or a job loss—the lack of savings combined with high credit usage can create a financial crisis. Without a financial cushion to fall back on, this person might have to rely even more on credit, leading to a cycle of debt that's difficult to escape.

The Danger of Underestimating Risk

Optimism bias doesn't just affect our savings habits; it also influences how we use credit. For example, someone with optimism bias might take on a large loan or mortgage, assuming that their income will always remain stable or increase. They might overlook the possibility of interest-rate hikes or changes in their financial situation, leaving them vulnerable if circumstances change.

This can also lead to overextending credit limits. If you believe that you won't face financial difficulties, you might be more inclined to accept credit limit increases or apply for additional loans. Overextending like this can quickly spiral into unmanageable debt, especially if an unexpected event occurs that disrupts your financial plans.

ANCHORING

Anchoring is when we rely too heavily on the first piece of information encountered—the "anchor"—when making decisions. In the context of credit, anchoring can lead to poor decision-making, especially when it comes to understanding the true cost of borrowing.

The Temptation of Introductory Offers

Credit card companies often use anchoring to their advantage by advertising low introductory interest rates or enticing signup bonuses. For instance, a credit card might offer a 0% interest rate for the first six months, which can be a powerful anchor. Consumers fixate on this attractive offer and may overlook or downplay the long-term interest rate that kicks in after the promotional period ends.

Imagine you sign up for a credit card with a 0% introductory rate, planning to pay off a large purchase during this period. However, life gets busy, and the balance isn't paid off as planned. After six months, the interest rate jumps to 20%, and now you're paying significant interest on a large balance. The anchor—the initial 0% rate—has distorted your perception of the credit card's true cost, leading to potentially costly consequences.

The Danger of Focusing on the Initial Offer

Anchoring can also occur when negotiating loan terms. For example, if the first interest rate you're quoted is 5%, you might anchor on that rate and consider any lower rate to be a good deal, even if better options are available. Anchoring can lead to accepting less favorable terms simply because they seem better relative to the initial anchor.

To avoid the pitfalls of anchoring, you need to look beyond the initial offer and consider the full scope of the credit terms—understanding how interest rates might change, any fees involved, and the long-term cost of carrying a balance.

AVAILABILITY HEURISTIC

The *availability heuristic* refers to the inclination to assess the probability of events based on how readily examples are recalled. This cognitive bias can distort perceptions of risk and reward, particularly with credit management.

The Influence of Memorable Stories

The availability heuristic often manifests when we hear stories about others' financial successes or failures. For example, if you frequently hear stories about people using credit to make large purchases and paying off their debt with ease, you might assume that managing credit is straightforward and low risk. This perception can lead to underestimating the difficulties involved in handling significant credit card debt.

On the other hand, if someone close to you experiences financial hardship due to credit card debt, that story might weigh heavily on your mind, leading you to avoid using credit altogether—even in situations where it could be beneficial, such as building credit history or taking advantage of low-interest financing.

The Skewed Perception of Risk

The availability heuristic can also influence our perception of financial risks. For instance, if you've never personally experienced financial difficulties due to credit, you might downplay the risks of accumulating debt. Conversely, suppose you've heard numerous stories of people struggling with credit card debt. In that case, you might overestimate the likelihood that the same issue will happen to you, leading to overly conservative financial behavior.

To counteract the availability heuristic, seek out a broad range of information and consider both positive and negative outcomes. Relying on a single story or example can lead to biased decision-making that doesn't fully reflect the complexities of credit management.

RECOGNIZING AND COUNTERACTING COGNITIVE BIASES

Understanding cognitive biases is the first step in mitigating their impact on our credit behavior. Read on for some strategies to help recognize and counteract these biases.

Seek Out Diverse Information Sources

Relying on a single piece of information or one story can lead to skewed perceptions. Make it a habit to gather information from multiple sources before making financial decisions. Gathering information can help you see the bigger picture and avoid falling into the trap of anchoring or the availability heuristic.

Reflect on Past Financial Mistakes

Take time to reflect on past financial decisions, especially those that didn't turn out as planned. Consider whether cognitive biases like overconfidence or optimism played a role. Learning from these experiences can help you make more informed decisions in the future.

Challenge Your Assumptions

When making credit-related decisions, challenge your initial assumptions. For example, if you're considering a new credit card because of an attractive introductory rate, ask yourself, *What happens after the promotional period ends? Can I afford the higher interest rate?* By questioning your assumptions, you can avoid the pitfalls of anchoring and make more informed choices.

As you can see, cognitive biases are powerful forces that can subtly yet significantly influence our financial decisions, particularly in how we manage credit. Overconfidence bias can lead us to believe we can handle more debt than is realistically manageable, resulting in financial overextension. Optimism bias might make us underestimate the likelihood of negative financial events, leaving us unprepared for potential setbacks and overly reliant on credit. Anchoring can cause us to focus too heavily on initial offers, such as low introductory interest rates, while neglecting the long-term costs that come after the promotional period ends.

Meanwhile, the availability heuristic can skew our perception of credit risks and rewards based on the most readily available examples rather than a balanced view of the potential outcomes.

If you understand these biases, you can start to recognize when they are influencing your decisions. This awareness is the first step in mitigating their effects.

In the next chapter, you'll learn about the psychology of spending. Here, we'll explore why we spend the way we do, the emotional triggers behind impulsive purchases, and how to develop healthier spending habits. Understanding the psychology of spending is key to gaining control over our financial lives and ensuring that our spending aligns with our long-term financial goals.

CHAPTER 7

THE PSYCHOLOGY OF SPENDING

Spending money is an activity we engage in daily, often without giving much thought to the motivations behind our purchases. Yet, our spending habits are far from arbitrary—they are shaped by our emotions, social influences, and cognitive biases. Understanding the psychology behind why we spend the way we do can allow us to make more mindful financial decisions, leading to better financial outcomes. In this chapter, we'll explore the psychological triggers that drive spending, examine the influence of social and cultural factors, and provide strategies for recognizing and controlling impulsive spending.

EMOTIONAL TRIGGERS AND FINANCIAL DECISIONS

Emotions play a role in financial decision-making, leading us to make choices that do not align with our rational financial goals. While we may strive to make logical, well-thought-out financial decisions, our emotions frequently guide our spending behavior, sometimes in ways that can undermine our financial stability.

The Emotions Behind Spending

Consider a time when you made an impulse purchase. Perhaps you were feeling stressed after a long day at work and decided to treat yourself to something nice, whether it was a new outfit, a fancy dinner, or a gadget you didn't really need. At that moment, the act of spending provided a sense of relief or reward—a temporary emotional boost that felt good but may have come with financial consequences.

This type of spending is driven by emotional triggers—specific feelings or states of mind that prompt us to spend money. Common emotional triggers include stress, anxiety, loneliness, boredom, and even happiness. When we're in these emotional states, we're more likely to make purchases that we might later regret, especially if those purchases exceed our budget or add to our debt.

Retail Therapy: A Double-Edged Sword

One of the most well-known examples of emotion-driven spending is "retail therapy," where shopping is used as a way to cope with negative emotions such as stress, anxiety, or depression. The term itself suggests that shopping can serve as a form of therapy, offering temporary relief from emotional discomfort.

Retail therapy often involves buying items on impulse—clothing, accessories, electronics, or other nonessential goods. The immediate gratification of making a purchase can provide a momentary sense of control or happiness, but this feeling is usually short-lived. Once the initial excitement wears off, the underlying emotions may return, sometimes accompanied by feelings of guilt or regret over the money spent.

Consider this example: After a particularly stressful week at work, you find yourself at the mall. The allure of a new designer handbag catches your eye. At the moment, buying the handbag feels like a well-deserved reward—a way to treat yourself for enduring the stress. You swipe your credit card without much thought, feeling a rush of satisfaction. But later, as you review your finances, the reality sets in: The handbag was expensive, and you've added to your credit card balance, which you were already struggling to pay off.

The problem with retail therapy is that it often leads to unnecessary spending and accumulating debt. While the act of shopping may provide short-term emotional relief, it can have long-term financial consequences that add to your stress and anxiety, creating a vicious cycle.

SOCIAL AND CULTURAL FACTORS

Our spending habits are not only influenced by our emotions but also by the social and cultural contexts in which we live. The way we manage credit and debt is connected with the values, norms, and expectations of our society, family, and peer groups.

The Role of Social Comparison in Credit Spending

Social comparison—the process of comparing ourselves to others —is a powerful force in shaping our spending behavior. We often look to our peers, friends, and even strangers as benchmarks for how we should live, what we should own, and how we should spend our money. This comparison can drive us to make purchases that align with the perceived norms of our social circle, even if those purchases are beyond our means.

For instance, imagine you're part of a group of friends who frequently dine at upscale restaurants, travel to exotic destinations, and wear the latest fashion trends. To fit in and maintain your social status within the group, you feel pressured to spend in similar ways, even if it means using credit to finance these luxuries. The desire to keep up with others can lead to overspending and accumulating debt as you prioritize social acceptance over financial prudence.

Cultural Attitudes Toward Debt and Saving

Cultural attitudes toward money, debt, and saving also play a great role in shaping our financial behavior. In some cultures, debt is viewed as a necessary tool for achieving financial goals, such as buying a home or funding a business. In others, debt is seen as something to be avoided at all costs, with a strong emphasis on saving and living within one's means.

These attitudes can influence how we approach credit and debt management. For example, in a culture that values financial independence and frugality, people may be more cautious about taking on debt and more disciplined about saving. In contrast, in a culture where credit is widely accepted and even encouraged, there may be a greater tendency to rely on credit for everyday expenses, leading to higher levels of debt.

The Influence of Family and Community on Credit Practices

Our family and community also shape our financial behaviors, often from a young age. The financial habits we observe in our parents, siblings, and other close relatives can leave a lasting impression on how we manage money as adults. If you grew up in a household where credit was used freely and debt was considered normal, you might be more inclined to adopt similar practices. Conversely, if your family emphasized saving and avoiding debt, you might be more cautious in your use of credit.

Community norms can also influence credit behavior. In communities where conspicuous consumption—publicly displaying wealth through material possessions—is valued, there may be social pressure to spend on luxury items, even if it means going into debt. On the other hand, in communities that prioritize financial security and modesty, there may be a greater emphasis on living within one's means and avoiding unnecessary debt.

EMOTIONAL SPENDING

Emotional spending occurs when we make purchases based on our emotions rather than our needs or financial goals.

The Emotional Spending Cycle

Emotional spending can create a cycle that is difficult to break. For example, you might feel bored and decide to go shopping as a way to fill the emotional void. The act of making a purchase provides a temporary boost in mood, but this is often followed by feelings of guilt or regret, especially if the purchase was unnecessary or beyond your budget. These negative feelings can then lead to more emotional spending as a way to cope, perpetuating the cycle.

A common example of emotional spending is celebrating a personal achievement, such as a promotion at work, with extravagant purchases. While it's natural to want to reward yourself for your hard work, it's important to ensure that the celebration doesn't lead to overspending or increased debt. For instance, splurging on a luxury vacation or a high-end piece of jewelry might bring temporary joy, but if it exceeds your budget, it can result in financial stress down the road.

TECHNIQUES FOR EMOTIONAL REGULATION

Recognizing the emotional triggers behind your spending is the first step in managing emotional spending. Once you're aware of these triggers, you can take steps to regulate your emotions and make more rational financial decisions.

Delayed Gratification

As mentioned in previous chapters, delayed gratification refers to the capacity to forego immediate pleasures in pursuit of a more substantial reward in the future. Cultivating this skill can mitigate impulsive spending tendencies and enhance your focus on achieving long-term financial aspirations.

Implementing a "cooling-off period" before making discretionary purchases is a great strategy for delayed gratification. For example, if you're tempted to buy a new gadget or piece of clothing, commit to waiting 24 hours before making the purchase. During this time, consider whether the item is truly necessary and whether it aligns with your financial goals. Often, the desire to buy will diminish, and you will decide that the purchase isn't as important as it initially seemed.

Another strategy is to set financial goals that require saving over time, such as building an emergency fund or saving for a down payment on a home. If you focus on these long-term goals, you can motivate yourself to delay gratification and avoid impulsive spending.

Budgeting

As mentioned in previous chapters, creating and sticking to a budget is one of the most effective ways to manage your finances and reduce emotional spending. A budget provides a clear plan for how you will allocate your income toward expenses, savings, and discretionary spending.

When creating a budget, consider including a "fun money" category for discretionary spending. Setting aside this money allows you to enjoy occasional treats or rewards without feeling guilty, as long as you stay within the allocated amount. Knowing that you have a designated budget for discretionary spending can also reduce the urge to make impulsive purchases, as you'll have already planned for and accounted for those indulgences within your financial framework.

To make your budget more effective, consider the following tips:

- **Use a budgeting application:** Platforms such as Mint, YNAB (You Need a Budget), or detailed personal finance spreadsheets (such as the one at the end of this book) can assist you in monitoring your expenses in real time and enhance your financial accountability.
- **Review your budget regularly:** Financial situations change, so it's important to revisit and adjust your budget as needed. This will help you stay on track with your goals and adapt to any new financial challenges or opportunities.
- **Set specific, measurable goals:** Instead of vaguely aiming to "spend less," define clear objectives, such as "reduce dining out expenses by 20% this month" or "save $200 for an emergency fund by the end of the quarter."

Understanding the psychology of spending is key to gaining control over your financial behavior. Our spending habits are deeply influenced by emotional triggers, social and cultural factors, and cognitive biases. By becoming aware of these influences, we can begin to make more mindful and rational financial decisions.

The good news is that by recognizing these influences, we can take steps to manage them. Techniques such as delayed gratification and many more can help us regulate our emotions, make more thoughtful spending decisions, and maintain better control over our credit and finances.

CHAPTER 8

THE ROLE OF HABITS IN CREDIT MANAGEMENT

K nowing how to manage credit effectively is essential, but it's not the only factor that determines success. Habits— the automatic behaviors we repeat daily—play an important role in shaping our financial lives. Whether it's paying bills on time, avoiding impulse purchases, or monitoring our credit reports, the habits we form can either support or sabotage our financial goals. Let's explore the psychology of habit formation, the impact of positive financial habits, and the strategies for breaking negative ones. With this information, you can develop routines that lead to better credit management.

THE PSYCHOLOGY OF HABIT FORMATION

Habits are behaviors that have become automatic through repetition. They are the brain's way of conserving energy by turning repeated actions into routines that require minimum conscious thought. This automaticity is both a blessing and a curse—while it allows us to perform daily tasks efficiently, it can also lead us to repeat behaviors that are not in our best interest, particularly when it comes to managing credit.

How Habits Are Formed

The process of habit formation can be broken down into three key components: the cue, the routine, and the reward. This cycle, often referred to as the *habit loop*, is the foundation of how habits are created and maintained.

1. **Cue:** The cue serves as the catalyst that starts the habit. It could be a time of day, an emotional state, or a specific situation. For example, receiving a bill in the mail might serve as a cue to pay it immediately.
2. **Routine:** The routine is the action you take in response to the cue. If paying the bill as soon as you receive it is your routine, this behavior becomes more ingrained over time.
3. **Reward:** The reward serves as a positive reinforcement that solidifies the habit. In this case, the reward might be the satisfaction of knowing you've avoided a late fee and maintained a good credit score.

Through repetition, the brain begins to associate the cue with the routine and the reward, eventually leading to the behavior becoming automatic. Once a habit is formed, it requires little conscious effort to maintain, which is why habits can be so powerful in shaping our financial behavior.

The Challenge of Changing Habits

While forming positive habits is beneficial, breaking negative ones can be challenging. Habits are deeply ingrained in our neural pathways, making them resistant to change. However, by understanding the habit loop, we can begin to disrupt negative habits and replace them with more constructive behaviors.

For instance, if your habit is to ignore your credit card statements until the due date, the cue might be the email notification that the statement is available. The routine is to dismiss the email without reviewing the statement, and the reward is avoiding the stress of confronting your spending. To change this habit, you could establish a new routine in which the cue (the email notification) prompts you to review the statement immediately. The reward could be the peace of mind that comes from being aware of your spending and catching any errors early.

POSITIVE FINANCIAL HABITS

Developing positive financial habits is essential for effective credit management. These help you stay organized, avoid unnecessary debt, and maintain good credit health. Let's explore some of them.

Regular Budgeting

One of the most important habits for managing credit is regular budgeting. Remember that budgeting involves tracking your income and expenses to ensure that you're living within your means and allocating funds appropriately.

For example, if you notice that you're consistently spending more on dining out than you've budgeted for, you can make a conscious effort to cut back on that area. This helps prevent the need to rely on credit to cover everyday expenses, which can quickly lead to debt accumulation.

To make budgeting a habit, set aside a specific time each week or month to review your finances. Use budgeting tools or apps to simplify the process and keep yourself accountable. Over time, regular budgeting becomes second nature, helping you maintain control over your finances.

Saving

Another crucial financial habit is saving regularly. Whether it's for emergencies, future needs, or specific financial goals, saving money is a key component of financial health. By building a habit of saving, you create a financial cushion that can protect you from unexpected expenses and reduce your reliance on credit.

One effective strategy for developing a saving habit is setting up automatic transfers from your checking account to your savings account each time you receive a paycheck, ensuring that you're consistently setting aside money before you have the chance to spend it. The habit of saving regularly not only strengthens your financial security but also provides peace of mind, knowing that you're prepared for the future.

Monitoring Credit

Regularly monitoring your credit is another habit that can have a positive impact on your financial health. If you check your credit reports and scores on a regular basis, you can track your progress, identify potential issues early, and take corrective action, if necessary.

For instance, if you notice an unexpected drop in your credit score, reviewing your credit report might reveal an error or unauthorized activity that needs to be addressed. Monitoring your credit also keeps you informed about your debt levels and credit utilization, helping you make informed decisions about how to manage your credit.

To make credit monitoring a habit, set a reminder to check your credit report at least once a quarter. Many financial institutions offer free credit-monitoring services that can alert you to changes in your credit report, making it easier to stay on top of your credit health.

BREAKING BAD FINANCIAL HABITS

While developing positive financial habits is essential, it's equally important to identify and break negative financial habits that can undermine your credit management efforts. Let's explore some common bad habits.

Impulse Spending

Impulse spending is one of the most common negative financial habits. It involves making unplanned purchases based on immediate desires rather than thoughtful consideration. This behavior can quickly lead to overspending and accumulating debt, especially if you're using credit to finance these purchases.

To break the habit of impulse spending, consider implementing a waiting period before making any significant purchase. For example, commit to waiting 24 hours before buying anything that wasn't already on your shopping list. This gives you time to evaluate whether the purchase is truly necessary and how it fits into your budget.

Another strategy is to identify the emotional triggers that lead to impulse spending, such as stress, boredom, or the desire for instant gratification. Knowing this, you can develop alternative ways to cope with them, such as taking a walk or finding a low-cost activity that brings you joy without derailing your finances.

Ignoring Statements

Another harmful financial habit is ignoring credit card and bank statements. When you don't review your statements regularly, you may miss important information, such as errors, unauthorized charges, or overspending in certain categories, leading to missed payments, higher interest charges, and a decline in your credit score.

To break this habit, make it a point to review your statements as soon as they become available. Set aside time each month to go through your statements line by line, ensuring that all charges are accurate and within your budget. If you find any discrepancies, address them immediately by contacting your credit card company or bank.

Minimum Payments

Paying only the minimum payment on your credit cards is another bad habit that can lead to long-term financial problems. While it may seem like a convenient way to manage your finances, paying only the minimum can result in higher interest charges and a longer repayment period, ultimately costing you more in the long run.

To break this habit, commit to paying more than the minimum payment each month. If possible, aim to pay off your entire balance to avoid interest charges altogether. If paying off the full balance isn't feasible, focus on paying as much as you can afford, especially on high-interest cards.

Another strategy is to prioritize paying off one card at a time, starting with the one with the highest interest rate. This approach, known as the *avalanche method*, can help you reduce your overall debt more quickly and save money on interest.

TOOLS AND TECHNIQUES FOR HABIT CHANGE

Changing financial habits—whether developing positive ones or breaking negative ones—requires intentional effort and the right tools. Let's look at some effective strategies.

Setting Goals

Setting clear, achievable financial goals is a great way to motivate yourself to change your habits. Goals provide a sense of direction and purpose, helping you stay focused on what you want to achieve. Whether it's paying off a certain amount of debt, building an emergency fund, or improving your credit score, having specific goals can drive you to adopt the habits necessary to reach them.

Reward Systems

Rewarding yourself for meeting financial targets can reinforce positive habits and make the process of habit change more enjoyable. Rewards don't have to be extravagant or expensive; they can be simple gestures that bring you joy and acknowledge your progress.

For example, if you successfully stick to your budget for a month, treat yourself to a small reward, such as a favorite meal or a relaxing activity. The key is to choose rewards that motivate you and reinforce positive behavior without derailing your financial goals.

Accountability

Having an accountability partner or working with a financial advisor can be extremely helpful in maintaining positive financial habits and breaking negative ones. Accountability adds an external layer of commitment, making you more likely to stay on track with your financial goals and habits.

The Role of Accountability Partners

An accountability partner can be anyone from a trusted friend or family member to a colleague, as long as they have aligned financial aspirations or can offer candid insights and constructive criticism. You can schedule regular check-ins, during which you discuss your progress, challenges, and any adjustments needed to stay on course. For example, you might agree to meet monthly to review your budget, discuss any impulse purchases, and celebrate achievements like paying off a credit card or sticking to a savings plan.

Having someone to support you and hold you accountable can make the process of habit change feel less isolating and more manageable. It also provides an opportunity for mutual learning and encouragement, as you can share strategies, insights, and experiences.

An important aspect of having an accountability partner is setting clear goals and expectations right from the start, which ensures that both you and your partner understand what success looks like. For instance, if your goal is to save a certain amount each month, be specific about how much that is and what strategies you'll use. You might decide to cut back on dining out or bring lunch to work instead. Regularly reviewing these goals keeps both of you on the same page, allowing you to adjust them if circumstances change. Openly discussing what's working and what isn't builds a layer of trust.

Another benefit of partnering up is the chance to learn from each other's mistakes. Everyone encounters challenges on their way to finding better financial health. Sharing these experiences can prevent others from repeating the same missteps. For example, if your partner fell for a sales pitch and bought something they didn't need, you can discuss how to recognize and avoid similar situations. This kind of candid conversation not only strengthens your bond but also enriches both of your experiences as you navigate your financial landscapes together.

Keeping the communication lines open is essential for a successful partnership. This could mean texting each other in between your scheduled meet-ups when something significant occurs. If one of you manages to stick to the budget for a couple of weeks or encounters an unexpected expense, sharing those moments helps maintain motivation and accountability. It also reinforces that neither of you is alone in your journey. Finding a reliable way to check in, whether through a shared app, an email, or simple calls, ensures that you're both engaged with each other's progress regularly.

Finally, it's crucial to celebrate even the small wins. Each achievement, no matter how minor, deserves recognition. When you or your partner accomplish something—whether it's saving the targeted amount or managing an unexpected expense effectively —take the time to acknowledge it. You might plan a small treat or a fun outing to mark the victory. Celebrating creates a positive feedback loop, encouraging both of you to keep moving forward. Acknowledgment of hard work doesn't just foster a good sense of achievement; it also builds a strong foundation for continuing together.

Working With a Financial Advisor

Consider enlisting the expertise of a financial advisor for a more structured approach. They can assist you in establishing attainable financial objectives, devising a strategy to reach those goals, and offering continuous support and accountability throughout the process. They can also offer expert advice on more complex financial matters, such as investment strategies, retirement planning, and debt management.

A financial advisor can help you identify any negative habits that are hindering your progress and suggest practical steps to address them. For example, if you struggle with impulse spending, your advisor might recommend specific budgeting tools or techniques to help you stay within your spending limits. They can also help you set up automatic savings plans or debt-repayment schedules, making it easier to stick to your goals.

As you can see, habits are the building blocks of our financial behavior. Whether they are positive or negative, the habits we form around credit management have a significant impact on our financial health and overall well-being.

Positive financial habits, such as regular budgeting, saving, and monitoring credit, can lead to better credit management and long-term financial success. On the other hand, negative habits such as impulse spending, ignoring statements, and making only minimum payments can create a cycle of debt and financial stress.

The good thing about habits is that they can be changed. With the techniques you learned in this chapter, you can develop new habits that are in line with your financial aspirations. Remember that it also takes time, effort, and consistency, but the rewards are well worth it—a more secure financial future and the peace of mind that comes with knowing you are in control of your credit and your financial destiny.

However, habits are just one piece of the puzzle. To achieve true financial mastery, we need to go deeper into the psychological strategies that can help us manage credit more effectively. In the next chapter, we will look at techniques like cognitive restructuring and behavioral interventions that can help you overcome cognitive biases and emotional triggers, leading to more rational and successful financial decisions.

HELP OTHERS USE MONEY TO GAIN CONTROL OVER THEIR FINANCIAL WELL-BEING

The ability to do what you want, when you want, with who you want, for as long as you want to, pays the highest dividend that exists in finance.

— MORGAN HOUSEL

In your reading journey thus far, you have seen how spending is inexorably linked to psychological factors. I have demonstrated that the reasons for negative habits like impulse buying, delaying financial planning, and living above one's means are often a product of our life experiences, financial education, and habits.

We also delved deeper into the psyche, revealing how emotions such as fear or anxiety and cognitive biases—the filters through which we view the world—can lead us to make decisions we later regret. The good news is that neither our environment nor our past defines our long-term relationship with money.

In the previous chapter, I explained how bad financial habits can be broken by changing your response to cues. In an average of a little over two months, most people can break a bad habit and replace it with a positive one. Implementing simple yet highly effective systems like waiting at least 24 hours before making a purchase can have a huge impact on your ability to curtail impulse buying—and on your financial future as a whole. You have also seen how finding other ways to reward yourself for smart financial behavior can give you a big confidence boost—and this can have a far-reaching effect on the way you manage money. If you find that this book is helping you take steps to manage your finances wisely, I hope you can share your opinion with others who are seeking guidance.

By leaving a review of this book on Amazon, you'll help new readers understand that changing the way they think about money can dramatically improve their financial well-being.

Thank you for sharing your thoughts. Here's to a future filled with sound financial decisions and time spent doing what you love.

Scan the QR code below

CHAPTER 9

STRATEGIES FOR PSYCHOLOGICAL MASTERY IN CREDIT MANAGEMENT

Mastering credit management means more than understanding interest rates or knowing how to budget; you need to develop the psychological tools and strategies that allow you to face the complexities of personal finance with confidence and clarity. With psychological insights and practical financial techniques, you can achieve a level of mastery that not only improves your credit health but also allows you to make smarter, more intentional financial decisions.

MINDFULNESS AND FINANCIAL AWARENESS

Mindfulness, often associated with meditation and stress reduction, is a powerful tool when applied to financial management. Being mindful of your financial behaviors and decisions means being fully present and aware of your actions, understanding the motivations behind them, and making deliberate choices that align with your financial goals.

Awareness Practices

One of the first steps toward psychological mastery in credit management is cultivating financial awareness. Consider regularly reflecting on your financial decisions and their underlying motivations. Ask yourself questions like:

- Why am I choosing to spend money on this particular item?
- What emotions or thoughts are driving this financial decision?
- How does this choice support my long-term financial objectives?

By asking these questions regularly, you begin to build a habit of financial self-awareness, which helps you recognize patterns in your spending, saving, and credit use. For example, you might notice that you tend to make impulsive purchases when you're stressed or that you're more likely to ignore your budget when you're feeling confident about your financial situation. Understanding these patterns allows you to make adjustments before they lead to negative financial outcomes.

The 50/30/20 Rule

The 50/30/20 rule is a simple budgeting strategy that helps you manage your money effectively by dividing your income into three categories: needs, wants, and savings. According to this rule, 50% of your income should go toward essential expenses like housing, utilities, groceries, and transportation. The next 30% is allocated to discretionary spending—things you enjoy but aren't necessary, such as dining out, entertainment, and hobbies. Finally, 20%

should be directed toward savings and debt repayment, helping you build financial security and achieve long-term goals.

To apply the 50/30/20 rule, start by calculating your monthly income and then break it down according to these percentages. Doing so will provide a clear framework for balancing your spending while ensuring that you prioritize savings and avoid overspending on nonessential items. Adjust the percentages if needed, but aim to keep savings a part of your budget to support future financial stability.

Continuous Financial Education

One of the most effective strategies of financial awareness is to stay informed and continuously educate yourself about personal finance. The financial world is constantly evolving, with new products, regulations, and strategies emerging all the time.

Learning Resources

There are countless resources available to help you deepen your understanding of personal finance and credit management. Books, online courses, podcasts, and financial workshops offer valuable insights into topics such as budgeting, investing, debt management, and credit building.

Consider dedicating time each week to learning about personal finance. Whether it's reading a chapter from a financial book, taking an online course, or listening to a finance podcast during your commute, continuous education helps you stay informed and make better financial decisions.

Staying Updated

In addition to ongoing education, it's important to stay updated on changes in the credit industry and financial regulations. New laws, policies, and market trends can impact your credit and overall financial health, so staying informed helps you adapt to these changes proactively.

Subscribe to financial news outlets, follow industry experts on social media, and sign up for newsletters from reputable financial organizations. If you stay informed, you can anticipate potential challenges and opportunities, allowing you to adjust your financial strategies accordingly.

BUILDING A SUPPORT SYSTEM

Building a support system of professionals, peers, and communities can provide the guidance, motivation, and accountability needed to achieve your financial goals.

Financial Advisors

A financial advisor offers personalized advice adapted to your specific financial situation and goals. They can help you create a comprehensive financial plan, manage your debt, and develop strategies for improving your credit score.

When selecting a financial advisor, prioritize a certified professional with extensive experience who resonates with your financial beliefs. Frequent meetings with your advisor will keep you aligned with your financial objectives and offer valuable insights into intricate monetary issues.

Support Groups

Joining support groups or online forums focused on personal finance and credit management can also be incredibly beneficial. These communities offer a space to share experiences, ask questions, and learn from others who are dealing with similar financial challenges.

For example, you might join a Facebook group dedicated to credit repair, where members share tips on negotiating with creditors, disputing errors on credit reports, and managing debt. Engaging with these communities can provide you with practical advice, emotional support, and the motivation to stay committed to your financial goals.

PRACTICAL EXERCISES AND TOOLS

In addition to psychological strategies, practical tools and exercises help you stay organized, track your progress, and make informed financial decisions.

Credit-Monitoring Services

Regularly assessing your credit is crucial for sustaining strong credit health. Credit-monitoring services offer real-time insights into your credit reports and scores, notifying you of any alterations or potential concerns, such as identity theft or unauthorized credit checks.

Services like Credit Karma, Experian, and MyFICO offer free or subscription-based credit monitoring, allowing you to track your credit score over time and receive personalized recommendations for improvement.

Financial Planning

Creating and regularly updating a financial plan is a key component of psychological mastery in credit management. A financial plan outlines your short-term and long-term financial goals, along with the steps needed to achieve them.

Your financial plan should include goals related to debt repayment, saving, investing, and credit improvement. By breaking down these goals into actionable steps and setting deadlines, you create a roadmap that guides your financial decisions and keeps you focused on your objectives.

Achieving psychological mastery in credit management is about more than simply managing your money—it's about mastering the mindset and habits that lead to long-term financial success.

As you continue to refine these strategies and apply them to your daily financial life, you'll find that credit management becomes less of a challenge and more of an opportunity to build a secure and prosperous future. The way to financial mastery is ongoing, but with the right mindset and tools, you can achieve lasting financial stability and peace of mind.

Now that you've learned strategies for achieving psychological mastery in credit management, it's time to go into the practical side of maintaining good credit. In the next chapter, we'll explore the essential steps for establishing a strong credit history, the factors that influence your credit score, and the best practices for keeping your credit in top shape. Whether you're starting from scratch or looking to improve your existing credit, this chapter will provide you with the insights you need to build and maintain a solid credit foundation.

CHAPTER 10

BUILDING AND MAINTAINING GOOD CREDIT

G ood credit is a tool that can open doors to numerous opportunities, from securing a mortgage with favorable terms to qualifying for the best credit card offers. But building and maintaining good credit requires more than just a one-time effort —you need to adopt consistent habits and strategies that protect and enhance your credit profile over time. In this chapter, we'll explore the key factors that contribute to a strong credit score, including timely payments, managing credit utilization, diversifying credit, and employing long-term credit-building strategies.

TIMELY PAYMENTS

The base of good credit is making timely payments. Payment history is the single most significant factor in calculating your credit score, accounting for roughly 35% of your FICO score. Lenders want to see that you're reliable in repaying your debts, and a consistent record of on-time payments demonstrates this reliability.

The Importance of On-Time Payments

When you consistently make timely payments on your credit cards, loans, and other bills reported to credit bureaus, you actively enhance your credit history. On the flip side, delays in payments can seriously harm your credit score, particularly if they exceed a 30-day grace period. The longer you wait to make a payment, the greater the potential damage, and missed payments can linger on your credit report for as long as seven years.

Strategies for Ensuring Timely Payments

To maintain a spotless payment history, consider implementing these strategies:

Automatic Payments

Setting up automatic payments is one of the most effective ways to ensure your bills are paid on time. Most banks and credit card issuers offer the option to automatically withdraw the minimum payment or full balance from your checking account each month.

However, it's important to monitor your bank account to ensure that you have sufficient funds to cover the automatic payments. Overdrafts can lead to fees and potentially damage your credit if the payment fails.

Payment Reminders

If you prefer more control over when your payments are made, setting up payment reminders can be a useful alternative to automatic payments. Many banks and financial apps allow you to set up alerts that notify you when a payment is due. These reminders can be sent by email, text message, or push notification, giving you ample time to make the payment before the due date.

To make this strategy even more effective, consider setting reminders a few days before the actual due date, which ensures that you have enough time to address any issues, such as insufficient funds or an unexpected delay in processing.

MANAGING CREDIT UTILIZATION

Credit utilization, which measures the amount of credit you are using against your total credit limit, is an important element in sustaining a healthy credit score. This factor influences roughly 30% of your FICO score, making it the second-most-significant determinant after your payment history.

Understanding Credit Utilization

Credit utilization measures how much credit you are using relative to your available limits. To calculate this, take the sum of your current outstanding credit card balances and divide it by the total credit limits available to you. For instance, if you possess two credit cards with a combined limit of $10,000 and your total balance stands at $2,500, your credit utilization rate would be 25%.

A lower credit utilization rate signals to lenders that you manage your available credit wisely and avoid excessive borrowing. On the other hand, a high utilization rate can indicate to lenders that you may be excessively dependent on credit, potentially raising concerns about your financial habits.

Strategies for Managing Credit Utilization

To maintain a healthy credit utilization ratio, aim to keep it below 30%. The following strategies could help:

Paying Down Balances

One of the most straightforward ways to reduce your credit utilization is to pay down your existing credit card balances. To avoid paying interest and maintain a low credit utilization rate, make it a priority to settle your full balance each month, when possible. If you're carrying a balance, prioritize paying down the cards with the highest utilization first.

Increasing Credit Limits

Another effective method to enhance your credit utilization ratio is by raising your credit limits. If you maintain a solid payment history and possess a healthy credit score, consider asking your credit card provider for an increase in your credit limit. This approach allows you to decrease your utilization ratio, even if your spending patterns remain unchanged.

However, always approach this strategy with caution. A higher credit limit can be tempting, leading to increased spending. To avoid this pitfall, treat the increased limit as a tool for improving your credit score rather than as an opportunity to take on more debt.

Spreading Out Purchases

If you have multiple credit cards, consider spreading out your purchases across different cards rather than concentrating them on a single card. This approach helps keep the utilization of each individual card low, which can be beneficial for your overall credit score.

For example, instead of charging $1,000 to a card with a $2,000 limit (resulting in a 50% utilization on that card), you could split the expense between two cards with higher limits, keeping each card's utilization below 30%.

DIVERSIFYING CREDIT

Having a mix of different types of credit is another factor that can positively impact your credit score. This aspect of your credit profile accounts for about 10% of your FICO score and demonstrates to lenders that you can manage various forms of credit responsibly.

Understanding Credit Mix

Credit mix encompasses the various categories of credit accounts that you possess, including credit cards, mortgages, auto loans, and personal loans. Lenders prefer to see a balance between revolving credit—e.g., credit cards—and installment credit—e.g., loans—because this demonstrates a comprehensive and responsible approach to managing credit.

Strategies for Diversifying Credit

To build and maintain a strong credit mix, consider the following:

Responsible Management of Credit Cards

Credit cards function as a type of revolving credit; this allows you to borrow up to a predetermined limit, repay the borrowed amount, and then borrow again. When used judiciously—such as making timely payments and maintaining low balances—credit cards can enhance your credit score.

If you currently possess only one credit card, consider diversifying your credit by obtaining an additional card. However, exercise caution to avoid opening multiple accounts simultaneously, as this can decrease your average account age and negatively impact your credit score.

Incorporating Installment Loans

If your credit report mainly features credit card accounts, incorporating an installment loan, such as a vehicle loan or a personal loan, can enhance the diversity of your credit profile. Installment loans require fixed payments over a set period, and successfully managing this type of credit demonstrates to lenders that you can handle different credit obligations.

However, it's important to only take on installment loans that make sense for your financial situation. For example, don't take out a personal loan solely to improve your credit mix if you don't genuinely need the funds.

Becoming an Authorized User

Becoming an authorized user of another person's credit card can be a strategic approach to improve or rebuild your credit score. If you join another person's credit account, you can take advantage of their favorable payment record and responsible credit use, which can positively influence your credit score.

However, this strategy only works if the primary account holder manages their credit responsibly. Be sure to choose someone with a strong credit history and a low utilization ratio.

LONG-TERM CREDIT BUILDING STRATEGIES

Building and maintaining good credit is a long-term commitment that requires ongoing effort and vigilance.

Consistent Monitoring

Regularly monitoring your credit reports and scores is essential for maintaining good credit health. If you keep an eye on your credit, you can track your progress, identify potential issues early, and take corrective action, if necessary.

How to Monitor Your Credit

You can obtain a complimentary credit report once a year from each of the three primary credit agencies—Equifax, Experian, and TransUnion—by visiting AnnualCreditReport.com. Review these reports for accuracy and look for any discrepancies, such as incorrect account information or signs of identity theft.

In addition to annual credit reports, consider using a credit monitoring service that provides regular updates on your credit score and alerts you to any significant changes. Many credit card issuers offer free credit score tracking, making it easy to stay informed.

Addressing Issues Promptly

If you discover errors or discrepancies on your credit report, always address them promptly. Start by contacting the credit bureau that issued the report and the creditor associated with the error. Provide any necessary documentation to support your dispute and request that the error be corrected or removed.

Promptly correcting inaccuracies in your credit report can safe-guard your credit score from potential harm and guarantee that your credit history truly represents your financial habits.

While building and maintaining good credit is crucial, don't forget that mistakes can happen. Whether it's a missed payment, a maxed-out credit card, or a negative mark on your credit report, credit mistakes don't have to define your financial future. In the next chapter, you'll explore practical strategies for bouncing back from credit missteps, repairing your credit score, and regaining control of your financial life.

CHAPTER 11

RECOVERING FROM CREDIT MISTAKES

Financial setbacks are a common part of life, and credit mistakes can happen to anyone. A mistake can be a missed payment, a maxed-out credit card, or even a more serious financial misstep like defaulting on a loan. However, the good news is that recovering from credit mistakes is entirely possible. It requires a combination of psychological resilience and practical strategies to rebuild your credit and regain financial stability.

PSYCHOLOGICAL IMPACT OF FINANCIAL SETBACKS

Experiencing financial setbacks can be emotionally challenging. The stress of dealing with debt, the anxiety of seeing a drop in your credit score, and the sense of failure that often accompanies financial mistakes can take a significant toll on your mental well-being. That's why it's important to recognize and address these emotions as part of your recovery process.

Emotional Acceptance

The first step in recovering from credit mistakes is emotional acceptance. Acknowledge that financial setbacks happen and that they do not define your worth or future potential. Many people experience financial challenges at some point in their lives, and it's important to remember that you are not alone in this.

Instead of dwelling on the past or blaming yourself, focus on the present and future. Accepting your situation allows you to take constructive action rather than getting stuck in a cycle of guilt and regret. This acceptance means you're not excusing mistakes but, instead, understanding that setbacks are a natural part of life and that you can overcome them with the right approach.

Building Mental Resilience

Mental resilience is the ability to bounce back from adversity and maintain a positive outlook despite challenges. Building resilience is crucial for recovering from credit mistakes because it helps you stay motivated and focused on your long-term goals, even when the path seems difficult.

One way to build resilience is to reframe your mindset. Instead of viewing financial setbacks as failures, see them as opportunities to learn. Ask yourself what lessons you can take away from the experience and how you can apply them to improve your financial habits in the future.

Another important aspect of resilience is setting realistic expectations for your recovery. Rebuilding credit and paying off debt takes time, and you need to be patient with yourself throughout the process. Celebrate small victories along the way, such as making consistent payments or seeing a slight improvement in your credit score, to keep your motivation high.

SEEKING PROFESSIONAL HELP

Seeking professional help can provide you with the guidance, support, and expertise you need to manage your debt and improve your credit.

Credit Counseling

Credit counseling is a service that provides people with personalized advice and strategies for managing debt and rebuilding credit. Credit counselors are trained professionals who can help you create a debt management plan, negotiate with creditors, and develop a budget that works for your financial situation.

When working with a credit counselor, you'll typically begin by discussing your financial goals and challenges. The counselor will then review your credit report, income, and expenses to develop a customized plan for paying off your debt and improving your credit score. This plan may include strategies such as consolidating your debt, reducing interest rates, or creating a payment schedule that fits with your budget.

Credit counseling can be especially helpful if you're feeling overwhelmed by your debt or if you're unsure of how to start rebuilding your credit. The support and accountability provided by a credit counselor can make a significant difference in your recovery.

Financial Advisors

In addition to seeking credit counseling, collaborating with a financial advisor can yield essential insights and tactics for enhancing your financial health. A financial advisor can assist you in devising a thorough financial strategy that not only tackles your debt and credit issues but also matches your long-term aspirations, such as retirement savings, investment opportunities, or acquiring a home.

CREATING AND STICKING TO DEBT REPAYMENT PLANS

One of the most important steps in recovering from credit mistakes is creating a structured debt repayment plan. A well-thought-out plan can help you systematically pay off your debt, reduce interest costs, and demonstrate responsible credit behavior to lenders.

Structured Plans

A structured debt repayment plan outlines how much you will pay toward your debt each month, which debts you will prioritize, and the timeline for becoming debt-free. There are various strategies for establishing a repayment plan, with the "debt snowball" and "debt avalanche" methods being the most effective options.

- **Debt snowball:** The debt snowball strategy encourages people to prioritize the repayment of their smallest debts first while continuing to make minimum payments on larger obligations. After eliminating a smaller debt, the freed-up payment amount is then applied to the next-smallest debt. This method generates a motivational effect as it allows you to experience rapid success by tackling minor debts.

- **Debt avalanche:** In contrast, the debt avalanche approach emphasizes addressing debts with the highest interest rates at the outset. If people focus on these high-interest obligations, they effectively minimize the total interest paid, potentially leading to significant savings over time. This strategy is especially advantageous for those burdened with substantial high-interest debts, such as credit card liabilities.

Prioritizing Debt

When creating your repayment plan, you need to prioritize your debts based on factors such as interest rates, balances, and the potential impact on your credit score. High-interest debts, such as credit cards and payday loans, should generally be prioritized because they can quickly grow if left unpaid.

Additionally, consider the impact of each debt on your credit score. For example, missed payments on a mortgage or auto loan can have a more significant negative effect on your credit score than missed payments on a smaller personal loan. By prioritizing these critical debts, you can protect your credit score while working toward becoming debt-free.

Regular Payments

Consistency is key when it comes to debt repayment. Making regular, on-time payments not only helps you reduce your debt but also demonstrates responsible credit behavior to lenders. Over time, this can lead to improvements of your credit score and increase your chances of qualifying for better financial products in the future.

TOOLS FOR CREDIT REBUILDING

As you work to pay off your debt and improve your credit, several tools can help you rebuild your credit history, including a secured credit card and credit-builder loans.

Secured Credit Cards

A secured credit card requires you to make a cash deposit that serves as collateral. This initial deposit determines your credit limit; for instance, if you deposit $500, your credit available will also total $500. Secured credit cards are an excellent option for people with poor or no credit history because they allow you to build credit by making regular, on-time payments.

Credit-Builder Loans

Credit-builder loans are specialized financial products aimed at assisting people in establishing or improving their credit scores. When you take out a credit-builder loan, a modest sum of money is deposited into a secure account while you make consistent monthly repayments. After you complete the payment process, the funds are released to you, and your payment behavior is reported to credit bureaus, positively impacting your credit profile.

Credit unions, local community banks, and various online lending platforms often provide credit-builder loans. They are an effective tool for establishing a positive payment history and improving your credit score over time.

As we've explored in this chapter, recovering from credit mistakes involves both practical and psychological strategies. How can we prepare ourselves to make well-informed financial choices in the future? In the next chapter, you'll go into the importance of financial education and how understanding the psychological principles behind money management can lead to better financial outcomes.

CHAPTER 12

THE ROLE OF EDUCATION IN FINANCIAL PSYCHOLOGY

F inancial education is the base of financial decision-making and the development of healthy financial habits. In a world where financial products and services are becoming increasingly complex, the ability to face finances with confidence is more important than ever. Financial literacy—the knowledge and understanding of financial concepts and risks—allows people to make informed decisions that lead to long-term financial well-being.

THE IMPORTANCE OF FINANCIAL EDUCATION

Financial education helps people understand the complexities of personal finance, from budgeting and saving to investing and credit management. Without a solid foundation in financial literacy, people are more likely to make poor financial decisions, fall into debt, and struggle to achieve financial stability.

Financial Education as a Tool for Empowerment

Financial education provides the knowledge and skills needed to manage money effectively, which leads to greater confidence in making financial decisions, reducing the anxiety and stress often associated with financial matters.

For example, someone who understands the basics of credit management is less likely to incur high-interest debt or miss payments, thereby maintaining a healthy credit score. Similarly, a person who is educated about investing can make informed decisions about retirement savings, avoiding common pitfalls such as excessive fees or inappropriate risk levels.

Moreover, financial education helps people set realistic financial goals and develop strategies to achieve them. If you understand concepts such as compound interest, asset allocation, and the time value of money, you can plan for your future with greater clarity and purpose.

The Impact of Formal Financial Literacy Programs

Formal financial literacy programs, offered by schools, universities, nonprofit organizations, and government agencies, play a significant role in promoting financial education. These programs are designed to provide structured learning experiences that cover a wide range of financial topics, from basic money management to advanced investment strategies.

Financial Literacy in Schools

Introducing financial literacy at an early age is important for developing lifelong financial habits. Many schools have started to incorporate financial education into their curricula, teaching students the basics of budgeting, saving, credit, and debt. These lessons provide a foundation that students can build upon as they enter adulthood and begin managing their own finances.

For example, a high school financial literacy course might cover topics such as how to balance a checkbook, the importance of saving for emergencies, and the basics of credit scores. By the time students graduate, they have a better understanding of how to manage their money and avoid common financial mistakes.

However, the availability and quality of financial education in schools can vary widely. In some regions, financial literacy is a required part of the curriculum, while in others, it is offered only as an elective or not at all, underscoring the need for more widespread and consistent financial education in schools. Financial education ensures that all students have the opportunity to develop essential financial skills.

University Programs and Adult Education

But financial literacy doesn't stop at high school. Many universities offer courses and workshops focused on personal finance, investment, and entrepreneurship. These programs are particularly valuable for young adults navigating college's financial challenges, such as student loans, budgeting, and credit management.

For adults who may not have had access to financial education earlier in life, community colleges, extension programs, and nonprofit organizations often provide courses and workshops aimed at improving financial literacy. These programs are designed to be accessible and practical, offering hands-on learning experiences that can be applied immediately to everyday financial decisions.

Government Initiatives

Governments around the world recognize the importance of financial literacy and have implemented various initiatives to promote financial education. These initiatives often include public awareness campaigns, online resources, and partnerships with educational institutions and financial organizations.

The Financial Literacy and Education Commission (FLEC) leads the initiative to enhance financial literacy across the US, unifying the federal government's resources and strategies. FLEC's MyMoney.gov website provides a wealth of resources on topics such as budgeting, saving, credit, and retirement planning (U.S. Department of Treasury, n.d.). The Consumer Financial Protection Bureau (CFPB) provides essential resources and guidelines designed to empower consumers in making well-informed financial choices.

THE ROLE OF INFORMAL FINANCIAL EDUCATION

While formal financial literacy programs are important, informal financial education also plays a significant role in shaping financial behavior. This education occurs through everyday interactions, such as conversations with family and friends, online communities, and self-directed learning.

Learning From Family and Peers

Family and peers are often the first sources of financial education. From a young age, people observe and absorb the financial behaviors of those around them.

However, one must recognize that not all financial behaviors learned from family and peers are positive. For example, if parents struggle with debt or lack financial discipline, their children may internalize these behaviors, leading to similar challenges in adulthood. Therefore, it's crucial to seek out diverse perspectives and continue learning beyond what is observed in the immediate family.

Online Communities and Resources

The Internet has revolutionized access to financial education, offering a wealth of resources for people seeking to improve their financial literacy. Online platforms such as community forums, blogs, podcasts, and YouTube channels offer valuable knowledge on various financial subjects, including effective budgeting, strategic saving, astute investing, and comprehensive retirement preparation.

One of the benefits of online financial education is its accessibility. Anyone with an internet connection can access high-quality financial content at little to no cost. Additionally, online communities allow people to connect with others who share similar financial goals and challenges, creating a supportive environment for learning and growth.

Self-Directed Learning

Self-directed learning is the process of taking initiative in one's education. This approach allows people to adapt their learning to their specific needs and interests, whether it's understanding the stock market, learning about real estate investing, or mastering the art of budgeting.

To engage in self-directed learning, start by identifying your financial goals and the areas where you need more knowledge. Then, seek out resources that align with those goals. This could include reading books by financial experts, taking online courses, or attending workshops and seminars.

For instance, if you're interested in improving your investment skills, you might start by reading books on investing, such as Benjamin Graham's *The Intelligent Investor* or John C. Bogle's *The Little Book of Common Sense Investing*. You could then supplement your reading with online courses on platforms such as Coursera or Udemy or by attending local investment seminars.

Understanding the role of education in financial psychology is just one piece of the puzzle when it comes to achieving long-term financial health. Education equips you with the knowledge and tools necessary to make informed decisions, but the real power lies in applying that knowledge consistently over time. In the next chapter, we'll explore the importance of adopting a long-term view in your financial planning and decision-making. We'll look at strategies for building wealth, maintaining financial stability, and preparing for life's uncertainties. Whether you're saving for retirement, investing in the stock market, or simply trying to stay on top of your day-to-day finances, taking a long-term approach can help you achieve lasting success and peace of mind.

CHAPTER 13

THE LONG-TERM PERSPECTIVE ON FINANCIAL HEALTH

Maintaining financial health is not just about making smart decisions today; it means adopting a long-term perspective that guides your financial actions throughout your life. Financial health requires consistent effort, adaptability, and a commitment to ongoing learning and monitoring.

SETTING SHORT-TERM AND LONG-TERM FINANCIAL GOALS

Goals give you direction, help you stay motivated, and guide you in making financial decisions.

Short-Term Goals

Short-term financial goals are those that are typically more specific and immediate, providing quick wins that help build momentum toward larger financial objectives. Examples might include:

- **Paying off credit card debt:** Establishing a clear timeline to lower your credit card balance can significantly lower interest expenses and enhance your credit score. Divide this objective into actionable steps, such as committing to a fixed monthly payment or targeting one card at a time.
- **Creating an emergency fund:** Aim to accumulate a savings buffer equivalent to three to six months of living expenses in an easily accessible account. A buffer will act as a safeguard against unforeseen circumstances, such as job loss or medical emergencies.
- **Implementing a budget and spending adjustments:** Committing to developing and adhering to a well-structured budget can optimize your daily financial management.

Long-Term Goals

Long-term financial goals require more extensive planning and a greater degree of patience, but they are essential for building lasting financial health. Examples might include:

- **Buying a home:** Purchasing a home is one of the most significant financial decisions many people ever make. Setting a goal to save for a down payment, improve your credit score, and secure a favorable mortgage rate requires careful planning and discipline.
- **Retiring comfortably:** Retirement may seem distant, but planning for it early is key to ensuring that you have the financial resources you need in your later years. Setting a goal to contribute regularly to retirement accounts, such as a 401(k) or an IRA, can help you build a nest egg that supports your desired lifestyle in retirement.

- **Paying off student loans or other debts:** If you have student loans or other substantial debt, setting a long-term goal to pay them off can free up resources for other financial priorities. Doing this might involve creating a debt repayment plan that works with your income and financial goals.

CONTINUOUS MONITORING OF CREDIT REPORTS AND SCORES

Regularly monitoring your credit reports and scores is a critical practice for maintaining long-term financial health. With this, you can identify potential issues early, correct errors, and take steps to protect and improve your credit.

Regular Checks

Your credit report is a detailed record of your credit history, including information about your accounts, payment history, and any negative marks such as late payments or defaults.

As we have mentioned, we highly recommend you review your credit reports from each of the three primary credit bureaus—Equifax, Experian, and TransUnion—at least once every year. You're entitled to one free credit report per year from each bureau through AnnualCreditReport.com (AnnualCreditReport, n.d.).

Pay attention to these points when reviewing your credit report:

- **Account information:** Verify that all accounts listed are yours and that the balances and payment histories are accurate.

- **Credit inquiries:** Review any inquiries made by potential lenders to ensure that you recognize them and that they were authorized.
- **Negative marks:** Look for any late payments, collections, or other negative marks that could impact your credit score.

Dispute Resolution

If you find an error on your credit report, you must address it promptly. Errors can include incorrect account information, unauthorized accounts, or inaccurate payment histories. To solve an error, follow these tips:

1. **Contact the credit bureau:** Start by contacting the credit bureau that issued the report. You can typically file a dispute online, by phone, or by mail. Be sure to provide detailed information about the error and any supporting documentation.
2. **Contact the creditor:** If the error involves a specific account, reach out to the creditor as well. They may be able to correct the issue directly with the credit bureaus.
3. **Follow up:** After filing a dispute, monitor the status to ensure that it is resolved. The credit bureau is required to investigate and respond to your dispute within 30 days.

THE IMPORTANCE OF ADAPTABILITY AND RESILIENCE

Life is inherently unpredictable, and financial situations can change instantaneously due to factors like unemployment, health crises, economic recessions, or shifts in family roles. The ability to adapt to these changes and remain resilient in the face of setbacks is crucial for long-term financial success.

Financial Adaptability

Financial adaptability involves being flexible and responsive to changes in your financial situation. This might mean adjusting your budget, revising your financial goals, or rethinking your investment strategy in response to new circumstances.

For example, if you experience a job loss, you may need to cut back on discretionary spending, prioritize essential expenses, and tap into your emergency fund. Alternatively, suppose you receive a windfall, such as a bonus or an inheritance. In that case, you might adjust your financial plan to allocate those funds toward paying down debt or increasing your savings.

Adapting to financial changes also involves staying informed about broader economic trends and how they might impact your financial situation. For instance, changes in interest rates, inflation, or tax laws can affect your savings, investments, and borrowing costs. With this, you can make proactive adjustments to your financial strategy to mitigate potential risks and capitalize on opportunities.

CASE STUDIES OF SUCCESSFUL LONG-TERM CREDIT MANAGEMENT

Learning from others' experiences can provide valuable insights and inspiration for managing your credit and financial health. The following case studies highlight people who have successfully managed and improved their credit over the long term.

Case Study 1: Rebuilding Credit After a Financial Setback

After experiencing a job loss, Jane found herself struggling to keep up with her bills. As a result, she missed several credit card payments, leading to a significant drop in her credit score (Push, 2022). Determined to rebuild her credit, Jane took a proactive approach by working with a credit counselor to create a debt management plan, which helped her catch up on missed payments and negotiate with creditors. She also opened a secured credit card to start rebuilding her credit history. She made small, manageable purchases and paid off the balance in full each month.

Over time, Jane's efforts paid off. Her credit score improved, and she qualified for a mortgage to purchase her first home.

Case Study 2: Long-Term Credit-Building for Future Goals

Sarah and Mark, a young couple, knew that they wanted to buy a home within the next five years. They recognized that having strong credit was important for obtaining a competitive mortgage rate, so they adopted a comprehensive, long-term approach to credit enhancement. They began by paying their credit card debts to lower their credit utilization ratio. Prioritizing high-interest loans, they employed a strategic method to reduce the overall interest burden effectively.

They used their credit cards regularly but always paid off the full balance each month. They also avoided opening new credit accounts unless absolutely necessary, to maintain a healthy average account age and limit hard inquiries (White, 2022).

With these strategies, Sarah and Mark were able to secure a mortgage with a low interest rate when they were ready to buy their home. Their disciplined credit habits not only helped them achieve their goal of homeownership but also set them up for ongoing financial success.

As you can see, taking a long-term perspective is essential for maintaining financial health and achieving your financial goals. But what does the future hold for credit management and financial psychology? In the next chapter, we'll explore emerging trends in the credit industry and how advances in psychological research are shaping the way we understand and manage credit. We'll explore the impact of technology, new credit scoring models, and the evolving role of behavioral economics in personal finance.

CHAPTER 14

THE FUTURE OF CREDIT AND PSYCHOLOGICAL RESEARCH

C redit management and psychological research are in a state of constant evolution, driven by technological advancements, new methods of credit scoring, and ongoing developments in behavioral economics. As these fields continue to grow and change, staying informed about emerging trends and research can allow people to face the future of credit more effectively.

EMERGING TRENDS IN CREDIT MANAGEMENT

Technological advances and innovative approaches to credit scoring are reshaping the landscape of credit management. These emerging trends offer both opportunities and challenges for people seeking to maintain or improve their credit health.

Technological Advances in Credit Management

Technology has transformed nearly every aspect of our lives, and credit management is no exception. From mobile banking apps to artificial intelligence, technological innovations are making it easier for consumers to manage their credit and make informed financial decisions.

Mobile Banking and Financial Apps

Mobile banking apps have revolutionized the way we manage our finances. These apps provide real-time access to account information, allowing users to monitor their spending, track their credit utilization, and make payments on the go. Many apps also offer features such as budgeting tools, spending alerts, and credit score monitoring, helping users stay on top of their financial health.

For example, apps like Mint allow users to create detailed budgets, set financial goals, and track their progress. Credit-monitoring services integrated into these apps provide regular updates on credit scores and offer personalized tips for improvement.

Artificial Intelligence (AI) and Machine Learning

Artificial intelligence (AI) and machine learning are increasingly being used in the credit industry to enhance credit scoring models, detect fraud, and provide personalized financial advice.

In the context of credit management, AI can help lenders assess creditworthiness more accurately by considering a broader range of data points, such as spending habits, social media activity, and online behavior. Using AI allows for more nuanced credit assessments and can open access to credit for people who may not have a traditional credit history.

Blockchain and Decentralized Finance (DeFi)

Blockchain technology and decentralized finance (DeFi) are poised to disrupt traditional credit systems by offering new ways to manage and access credit. Blockchain provides a secure and transparent way to record transactions, which can enhance the accuracy and integrity of credit reporting.

DeFi platforms, which operate on blockchain technology, allow users to borrow, lend, and invest without the need for traditional financial intermediaries. These platforms use smart contracts to automate transactions, reducing the need for credit checks and potentially expanding access to credit for underserved populations.

ALTERNATIVE CREDIT SCORING

Traditional credit assessment models, including FICO and VantageScore, primarily focus on key elements such as payment history, credit utilization ratios, and the overall duration of one's credit accounts. While these models have effectively assessed credit risk, they often exclude people who lack a traditional credit history, such as young adults, immigrants, and those who prefer to use cash.

In response to these limitations, alternative credit scoring methods are emerging that consider nontraditional data sources to evaluate creditworthiness.

Rent and Utility Payments

Some alternative credit-scoring models incorporate rent and utility payment histories into their assessments. For many people, rent and utility payments are significant monthly expenses, and a consistent payment history in these areas can be an indicator of creditworthiness. Companies like Experian Boost and Esusu have developed tools that allow consumers to include these payments in their credit reports, potentially improving their credit scores (Akin, 2023).

Social Media and Digital Footprints

Some lenders and fintech companies are exploring the use of social media data and digital footprints as part of the credit-scoring process. For example, a person's online behavior, such as their social media activity, e-commerce transactions, and even their mobile phone usage, can provide insights into their financial habits and reliability.

THE EVOLVING FIELD OF BEHAVIORAL ECONOMICS AND PSYCHOLOGY

Behavioral economics and psychology continue to show factors that influence financial behavior. As these fields evolve, new insights are emerging that can be applied to improve credit management practices.

New Insights in Behavioral Economics and Psychology

Behavioral economics combines principles of psychology and economics to understand why people make certain financial decisions, often revealing that these decisions are not always rational. Recent research by Egiyi and Ogbodo (2023) has provided new insights into how cognitive biases, emotions, and social influences impact credit management.

Loss Aversion and Credit Behavior

Loss aversion is the tendency to prefer avoiding losses over acquiring gains, which can greatly impact credit behavior. For example, people may be more motivated to pay off a debt when they perceive it as a way to avoid future losses (such as interest charges) rather than as a way to gain financial freedom.

This insight can be applied to credit management strategies by framing financial decisions in terms of loss avoidance. For instance, promoting the idea of "avoiding interest charges" rather than "saving money" may be more effective in encouraging timely debt repayment.

Present Bias and Credit Usage

As mentioned in previous chapters, this bias can lead to impulsive spending and the accumulation of credit card debt, as people may focus on the short-term gratification of a purchase rather than the long-term consequences of interest and debt.

Understanding present bias enables people to devise effective strategies to mitigate its effects. For instance, they can establish waiting periods before making sizable purchases or utilize automated savings systems to focus on long-term financial objectives.

PRACTICAL APPLICATIONS OF NEW RESEARCH

The insights from behavioral economics and psychology have practical applications in credit management, including nudge theory and gamification.

Nudge Theory in Credit Management

Nudge theory, a concept from behavioral economics, involves subtly guiding people toward better decisions without restricting their freedom of choice. In the context of credit management, nudges can be used to encourage positive financial behaviors.

For example, apps that provide spending alerts or suggest savings goals can nudge users toward more responsible credit usage.

Gamification and Financial Education

Gamification refers to the integration of game design principles into non-gaming environments to enhance motivation and build engagement among people. Financial education programs that use gamification techniques—such as rewards, challenges, and leaderboards—can make learning about credit management more interactive and enjoyable.

For instance, apps like Habitica turn financial goals into challenges that users can "level up" by completing tasks like paying off debt or sticking to a budget. This approach leverages the principles of behavioral psychology to make financial education more engaging and effective.

FUTURE RESEARCH DIRECTIONS

As the fields of credit management and psychological research continue to evolve, several key areas are emerging as important directions for future research. These areas have the potential to shape the future of credit management strategies and enhance our understanding of financial behavior.

The Impact of Digital Financial Platforms

With the rise of digital banking and fintech platforms, there is a growing need to study how these technologies impact financial behavior and credit management. Research in this area could explore how digital platforms influence spending habits, savings behavior, and credit utilization, as well as their role in promoting financial inclusion.

The Role of Mental Health in Credit Management

Mental health significantly impacts financial behavior yet is often overlooked in discussions about credit management. Future studies should examine how mental health issues—like anxiety, depression, and stress—impact financial decision-making processes. Understanding this connection could lead to more targeted interventions and support for people struggling with both mental health and financial challenges.

Ongoing research in these areas will have significant implications for credit management strategies. If people stay informed about the latest research findings, they and financial institutions can adapt their practices to better support credit health and financial well-being.

Staying informed about the future of credit and psychological research is key to maintaining financial health. But how can you take what you've learned and apply it to empower your overall financial well-being? In the next chapter, we'll bring together the principles and strategies discussed throughout this book, offering a comprehensive guide to achieving financial security.

CHAPTER 15

EMPOWERING FINANCIAL WELL-BEING

Your financial well-being means that not only do you have money, but you also feel secure and in control of your financial future. It's about knowing that you can handle the ups and downs of life without undue stress or anxiety. Throughout this book, we've explored the psychological principles of personal finance and credit management, offering insights and strategies to help you build a strong financial foundation. In this chapter, we'll summarize these key principles and provide strategies for achieving financial well-being.

THE IMPORTANCE OF A HEALTHY FINANCIAL MINDSET

At the core of financial well-being is a healthy financial mindset—it shapes how you think about money, how you manage it, and how you make financial decisions. A positive, growth-oriented mindset empowers you to take control of your finances, overcome challenges, and achieve your goals.

Cultivating a Growth Mindset

A growth mindset is the conviction that dedication and education can enhance your financial capabilities. Rather than perceiving financial obstacles as daunting barriers, a growth mindset motivates you to recognize them as valuable chances for development and insight.

To develop a growth mindset, start by accepting the idea that mistakes are part of the learning process. Instead of dwelling on past financial missteps, focus on what you've learned and how you can apply that knowledge to make better decisions in the future.

For example, if you've struggled with debt in the past, use that experience to develop stronger budgeting and spending habits. If you shift your focus from failure to growth, you can build confidence in your ability to manage your finances effectively.

Developing Financial Confidence

Financial confidence comes from understanding your financial situation, knowing your goals, and having a plan to achieve them. You feel empowered to make financial decisions without fear or uncertainty.

Building financial confidence starts with education. The more you know about personal finance and credit management, the more confident you'll feel in making decisions. Take the time to educate yourself through books, courses, and workshops. Stay informed about changes in the financial landscape and seek out resources that help you stay up-to-date.

In addition to knowledge, financial confidence arises from proactive steps. Establish clear financial objectives, have a practical budget, and pursue your goals with positivism. As you see progress, your confidence will grow, reinforcing your ability to manage your finances successfully.

A ROADMAP TO FINANCIAL EMPOWERMENT

Empowering your financial well-being requires a strategic, multi-step approach that integrates the psychological principles we've discussed throughout this book.

Step 1: Establish Defined Financial Objectives

Defining precise financial objectives serves as a step toward achieving economic empowerment. These objectives guide your focus and inspire commitment, ensuring you prioritize what truly matters.

Begin by distinguishing between immediate and future goals. Immediate targets could encompass settling credit card debts, creating an emergency savings fund, or setting aside funds for a getaway. In contrast, future aspirations might include purchasing a home, preparing for retirement, or eliminating student loan obligations.

After clarifying your objectives, deconstruct them into specific, actionable tasks. For instance, if your aspiration is to accumulate funds for a down payment on a home, calculate the monthly savings required and initiate automatic deposits into a separate savings account.

Step 2: Create a Budget and Stick to It

Budgeting serves as an essential tool for effectively managing your finances and reaching your objectives. It enables you to monitor your income and expenditures, ensuring that you remain within your financial boundaries while directing resources toward your priorities.

To begin crafting your budget, identify all sources of income alongside both your fixed and variable costs. Fixed costs, such as rent, mortgage payments, and insurance premiums, remain consistent each month. In contrast, variable costs—including groceries, leisure activities, and dining—can vary from month to month.

After compiling your income and expenses, allocate funds toward your financial aspirations. This may require reducing discretionary spending to create more room for savings or debt reduction. Leverage budgeting applications or tools to track your outlays and make necessary adjustments.

Adhering to your budget demands commitment, but the benefits you'll reap will make it worthwhile. Witnessing your savings increase and your debt diminish will impart a deep sense of achievement and empowerment.

Step 3: Build and Maintain Good Credit

Good credit is fundamental to achieving financial stability. It influences your capacity to obtain loans, acquire advantageous interest rates, and even impacts your eligibility for certain employment opportunities or rental contracts. Sustaining good credit demands ongoing diligence and care.

To preserve a strong credit profile, prioritize these essential elements:

- **Punctual payments:** Ensure that all bills are paid on or before their due dates. Delayed payments can have a debilitating effect on your credit score, so consider setting up automatic payments or calendar reminders to stay on track.
- **Credit usage:** Maintain a low credit-utilization ratio by utilizing only a minor percentage of your total available credit. It's advisable to keep this ratio below 30% to uphold a strong credit score.
- **Credit review:** Consistently assess your credit reports and scores to monitor your improvement and detect any potential discrepancies. If you uncover any inaccuracies, rectify them swiftly to safeguard your credit status.

If you're in the process of rebuilding your credit, think about leveraging secured credit cards or credit-builder loans. These financial tools can assist you in establishing a solid payment history and enhancing your credit standing over time.

Step 4: Continuously Educate Yourself

Financial education is an ongoing process that doesn't stop once you've achieved your goals. The financial world is constantly evolving, with new products, services, and regulations emerging all the time. Staying informed is key to adapting to these changes and making informed decisions.

Make a commitment to continuous learning by reading financial books, taking online courses, and attending workshops or seminars. Stay updated on the latest trends and research in personal finance and credit management. Engage with financial communities and networks to share knowledge and learn from others.

Step 5: Cultivate Resilience and Adaptability

Life is unpredictable, and financial setbacks are inevitable. The key to long-term financial well-being consists of two words: resilience and adaptability. Resilience allows you to bounce back from challenges, while adaptability enables you to adjust your financial strategies as needed.

To build resilience, focus on maintaining a positive mindset and viewing setbacks as opportunities for growth. If you experience a financial setback, such as job loss or unexpected expenses, take it as a chance to reassess your financial plan and make necessary adjustments.

Adaptability involves being flexible in your approach to financial management. As your life circumstances change, be willing to revise your goals, budget, and strategies. For example, if you receive a promotion or a raise, consider how you can allocate the extra income to achieve your long-term goals more quickly.

Empowering your financial well-being means you're taking control of your financial future. You're making intentional choices, setting clear goals, and taking proactive steps to achieve them. With the insights and strategies you've gained from this book, you have the tools you need to build a secure and prosperous financial future.

Remember, financial well-being requires ongoing effort, learning, and adaptation. But if you stay committed to your goals and apply the principles you've learned, you can create a life of financial freedom and peace of mind.

As we conclude this chapter, you'll want to recognize that looking for financial security can look different for everyone. For immigrants, building and improving credit scores presents unique challenges and opportunities. In the last chapter, we'll explore the specific strategies and resources available to help immigrants establish and grow their credit in a new country. Whether you're new to the financial system or looking to improve your existing credit, this chapter will provide practical guidance to help you achieve your financial goals in your new home.

CHAPTER 16

BUILDING AND IMPROVING CREDIT SCORES AS AN IMMIGRANT

This chapter is inspired from my own experience of credit management as an immigrant. I am happy to use the opportunity offered by this book, to share it with other immigrants, to help you manage your personal finance with confidence and decipher the credit system.

Moving to a new country is an adventure filled with opportunities, but it also has its fair share of challenges—especially in building a solid financial foundation. One of the biggest hurdles many immigrants face is understanding and facing the credit system, which often operates very differently from what you might be used to back home.

Here, we explore the steps to establish a credit score from the ground up—particularly for immigrants who are facing credit for the first time. This book is inspired by my journey as an immigrant from a country where credit scores aren't structured like they are in Western nations. From having no credit history to building one, and from avoiding credit cards to knowing their use—these are lessons I've learned firsthand.

My experience began with obtaining a secured credit card using an ITIN as a business owner, later evolving to a conventional credit card once I obtained an SSN. Now, I routinely receive offers for premium credit cards with substantial limits, car loans, mortgages, and personal loans from diverse lenders. I aim to share these insights with you in a practical, relatable manner.

But don't worry; building and improving your credit score is entirely within your reach, and this chapter will guide you through the process. Along the way, I'll touch on some unique aspects of the immigrant experience and point you to other parts of this book where you can go deeper into specific strategies and mindset shifts.

Improving a credit score is not just a financial challenge; it's a psychological one, as well. The process requires discipline, patience, and a willingness to confront and change financial behaviors. However, the psychological rewards of improving a credit score can be substantial, leading to increased confidence, reduced stress, and greater financial opportunities.

THE IMMIGRANT EXPERIENCE WITH CREDIT

Let's start with the immigrant experience, this requires adaptation and growth. However, when it comes to credit, the road can be a bit bumpy. Whether starting from scratch with no credit history, getting to grips with a new system, or overcoming the fear of taking on debt, these challenges can sometimes feel overwhelming. Every obstacle presents a chance for growth.

Starting From Scratch

Let's face it: Starting with no credit history can feel daunting. In many cases, the credit history you built back home doesn't follow you, leaving you to start from square one. But here's the silver lining—starting from scratch also means you have a clean slate to build a strong, positive credit history from the ground up.

Facing Cultural Differences

Cultural attitudes toward credit and debt can vary widely, and these differences can shape how you approach the credit system in your new country. In some cultures, using credit or taking on debt is frowned upon, leading to a preference for cash transactions. In others, credit might not play a significant role at all. But in your new home, understanding and using credit wisely is key to financial success. By learning about the local credit system, you can begin to navigate it with confidence, setting the stage for financial growth.

BUILDING FINANCIAL CONFIDENCE AS AN IMMIGRANT

Financial confidence is crucial, especially when you're facing a new financial landscape. While we'll touch on it here, remember that if you want to learn about how to build financial confidence, check out Chapter 15. It's packed with tips and strategies to help you feel more in control of your finances.

Overcoming Fear and Misinformation

It's completely normal to feel a bit intimidated by the credit system —especially if it's new to you. You might have heard horror stories or feel uncertain about how it all works. But here's the thing: Credit, when used responsibly, is a great tool. It's not something to be feared but rather something to be understood and managed wisely. To get more comfortable with the concept of credit and how it can work for you, remember to take a look at Chapter 2, where we discuss how to shift from fear to empowerment.

Understanding the Credit System

A solid understanding of the credit system is your ticket to building and improving your credit score. While this chapter offers an overview, you'll find a detailed breakdown of credit scores, reports, and the factors that influence them throughout this book.

Building a Support System

No one has to go it alone. Building financial confidence also means surrounding yourself with a support system—people who can offer guidance, advice, and encouragement. Whether it's financial advisors, community organizations, or fellow immigrants who've walked the same path, having a network can make a world of difference. Reach out, connect, and learn from those who've successfully built their credit.

Small Steps to Big Success

Small, consistent steps can lead to significant progress when it comes to building and improving your credit score. If you're looking for a detailed roadmap on how to take those steps and set achievable financial goals, Chapter 3 is the place to go—there is practical advice on everything from budgeting to keeping your credit utilization in check.

Mindset Shifts: From Fear to Empowerment

Building and improving your credit isn't just about understanding the mechanics—it means changing how you think about money and credit. Moving from a place of fear to a place of empowerment can completely change your finances. For a more detailed look at how to shift your mindset and embrace the learning process, turn to Chapter 2. It's all about helping you see credit not as something to fear but as a tool that can help you achieve your long-term goals.

PRACTICAL STRATEGIES FOR BUILDING CREDIT

While understanding the credit system and adopting the right mindset are crucial, it's the practical steps that will help you see real progress. Here are some strategies to help you build and improve your credit:

Obtaining a Secured Credit Card

As we mentioned previously, the first step to building your credit history is to obtain a secured credit card. This type of card is designed specifically for people with no credit history or poor credit. Here's how you can get one:

- **Research banks and credit unions:** Look for banks or credit unions that offer secured credit cards. Many of these institutions cater specifically to immigrants or people with no credit history.
- **Prepare your documents:** Depending on your immigration status, you may need different types of documentation. If you don't have a Social Security

Number (SSN), you can use an Individual Taxpayer
Identification Number (ITIN) to apply. Make sure you
have proof of income and identity.

- **Make the deposit:** A secured credit card requires a
  security deposit, which typically ranges from $200
  to $500.
- **Apply for the card:** Submit your application with the
  required documents and deposit. Once approved, you'll
  receive your secured credit card in the mail.

Tip: Start with a small credit limit, and use the card for everyday purchases like groceries or gas. This way, you can manage payments more easily and build your credit without overextending yourself.

Establishing a Budget

A budget is your financial blueprint. If you monitor your income and expenses, you guarantee that you live within your financial limits while strategically directing resources toward your financial objectives. For tips on creating and sticking to a budget, Chapter 3 has got you covered.

Making Payments on Time

Your payment history is the base of your credit score. Consistently making payments on time is the most effective way to build and maintain good credit. Set up reminders or alarms to help you stay on track.

Keeping Credit Utilization Low

Your credit utilization significantly impacts your financial well-being. Strive to maintain this ratio below 30%. To achieve this, consider implementing tactics such as making several payments throughout the month or asking for an increase in your credit limit.

Monitoring Your Credit Regularly

Monitoring your credit report is important for assessing your financial growth and identifying discrepancies promptly. You can obtain one free credit report annually from each of the three primary credit bureaus, so make it a routine to evaluate these reports and challenge any inaccuracies you find. For more detailed strategies on effectively tracking your credit, refer to Chapter 3.

Building and improving your credit score as an immigrant comes with its own set of challenges, but with the right knowledge, mindset, and support, it's entirely achievable. This chapter has highlighted some of the aspects of the immigrant experience, but don't forget to refer to previous chapters to refresh the tips and tricks.

Remember that you're not alone in this. Many immigrants have successfully built and improved their credit scores, and with the right approach, you can, too. Accept the process, stay committed, and remember that each step you take brings you closer to financial success in your new home.

Help Empower Others Through Financial Knowledge

As you come to the close of this book, I hope that you are keen to discover more about yourself and the psychological factors that shape the way you make, spend, and save or invest money. I also hope that this book sparks a lifelong curiosity about how to keep on top of your finances and make the most of the money you earn and save.

You have seen that maintaining good financial well-being involves embracing smart strategies like smart budgeting, setting goals, and practicing accountability. However, new developments and technologies mean that it pays to embrace lifelong financial learning. By staying updated, building a support system, and relying on reputable financial advisors, you can ensure that money is never a source of worry or stress. Before you start applying the many strategies we have discussed, however, I hope you can leave a short review so that others can find the path to a better future.

LEAVE A REVIEW!

Thank you for letting others know of the unique peace of mind that arises when you gain financial mastery.

Scan the QR code below

CONCLUSION

Congratulations on finishing this book! Now it's time to reflect on the key insights and strategies we've explored. This book has explored understanding numbers or mastering financial tools, all the while empowering you to take control of your financial future with confidence and a deep understanding of the psychological forces that shape your decisions.

Throughout this book, you learned about the looked at the complex relationship between psychology and finance, uncovering how our thoughts, emotions, and behaviors influence our financial outcomes. We've explored the importance of developing a healthy financial mindset, the role of cognitive biases in credit management, and the power of habits in shaping our financial behavior.

You also learned practical strategies for building and maintaining good credit, recovering from financial setbacks, and facing the credit system as an immigrant. These strategies are designed to be actionable and accessible, allowing you to make informed decisions and take meaningful steps toward achieving your financial goals.

From setting clear financial goals and creating a budget to understanding credit scores and managing debt, each chapter has served as a guide to financial well-being. If you integrate these insights into your daily life, you can create a solid foundation for long-term financial success.

One of the central themes of this book is the importance of integrating psychological and practical approaches to financial management. It's not enough to simply understand the mechanics of credit or budgeting; true financial knowledge comes from recognizing the psychological factors that influence our decisions and learning how to manage them effectively.

If you combine practical financial tools with a deep awareness of your own psychological tendencies, you can develop a more holistic approach to money management, allowing you to make decisions that align with your values and long-term goals, rather than being swayed by short-term impulses or external pressures.

For example, understanding the impact of cognitive biases like overconfidence or present bias can help you avoid common financial pitfalls and make more rational, informed choices. Likewise, learning how to develop the right mental attitude and acquiring the right skills can help you face any financial difficulty.

As we finish, know that this doesn't end here. The financial world is constantly evolving, and staying informed and adaptable is key to maintaining your financial health. Continue to seek out new knowledge, whether through books, courses, or conversations with others who share your financial goals.

Stay curious, stay proactive, and most importantly, stay committed to your financial goals. The insights and strategies you've gained from this book are tools that can help you build the life you want —one of financial freedom and security.

Thank you for joining me on this ride. I wish you continued success and financial empowerment.

INTERACTIVE ELEMENTS

QUIZ #1: FINANCIAL MINDSET

It's time for a quiz! As mentioned throughout the book, your financial mindset shapes how you approach money, savings, investments, and financial decisions. This quiz will help you understand whether you have an abundance mindset, scarcity mindset, fixed mindset, or growth mindset. Answer the questions honestly, and at the end, you'll receive feedback and tips to help you improve your financial outlook.

Quiz Questions

1. How do you feel when you think about money?

    A. Excited and confident
    B. Worried and anxious
    C. Indifferent or resigned
    D. Motivated to learn more

2. When you receive extra income, what is your first thought?

A. Invest it or save it for future opportunities.

B. Hold onto it tight because I might need it later.

C. It won't make much difference.

D. I use it to improve my current financial situation.

3. How often do you check your financial goals?

A. Regularly—I keep track of my progress.

B. Rarely—I'm more focused on day-to-day needs.

C. I don't really set goals.

D. Occasionally—especially when circumstances change.

4. When considering an investment, your primary concern is:

A. The potential for long-term growth

B. The risk of losing money

C. Whether it's worth the effort

D. Learning and growing throughout the experience

5. How do you approach budgeting?

A. It's an opportunity to plan for future success.

B. It's a necessity to avoid running out of money.

C. I find it difficult to stick to a budget.

D. It's a tool for improving my financial habits.

6. Do you think you have the power to change your financial circumstances?

A. Absolutely—with the right strategies
B. It's difficult but possible
C. Not really—things are as they are
D. Yes, with effort and learning

7. When faced with a financial setback, you:

A. See it as a learning opportunity
B. Worry about how it will affect your future
C. Feel discouraged and stuck
D. Analyze what went wrong and try to improve

8. How do you feel about taking financial risks?

A. I accept well-considered risks.
B. I strive to minimize exposure to uncertainty.
C. I'm open to risks if they come with learning opportunities.
D. I'm hesitant; I don't see the point.

9. When thinking about retirement, you:

A. Have a plan and are actively saving
B. Worry if you'll have enough to retire
C. Feel uncertain about the future
D. See it as a chance to achieve financial freedom

10. What do you think about debt?

A. It's a tool that can be managed wisely.

B. It's something to avoid at all costs.

C. It's a necessary burden.

D. It's manageable if approached strategically.

Scoring System

- **Every a:** 5 points
- **Every b:** 3 points
- **Every c:** 1 point
- **Every d:** 4 points

Result Interpretation

Score 40–50: Abundance Mindset

- You view money as a tool for growth and opportunity. You're confident in your financial decisions and are willing to take calculated risks. This mindset is conducive to long-term financial success, but be careful not to become overconfident or take on unnecessary risks.

Score 30–39: Growth Mindset

- You believe in your ability to improve your financial situation through learning and effort. You're open to new ideas and are proactive in your financial planning. Continue developing your financial knowledge and skills to fully realize your potential.

Score 20–29: Scarcity Mindset

- You tend to view money as limited and are often worried about not having enough. This mindset can lead to cautious financial behavior, which can be beneficial in avoiding debt but might also prevent you from taking advantage of opportunities. Work on building financial confidence and exploring new ways to manage money.

Score 10–19: Fixed Mindset

- You may feel stuck in your current financial situation and are unsure if change is possible. This mindset can limit your financial growth and prevent you from making proactive decisions. Consider challenging these beliefs and exploring how small changes in your financial habits can lead to improvements.

EMERGENCY FUND WORKSHEET

Monthly Expenses Calculation:

- Housing: $_____
- Food: $_____
- Transportation: $_____
- Insurance: $_____
- Debt Payments: $_____
- Other Essentials: $_____
- **Total Monthly Expenses: $_____**

Savings Goal:

- Select Target: [ ] 3 months [ ] 6 months [ ] 12 months [ ] Custom: _____
- **Total Savings Goal: $_____**

Savings Timeline:

- **Monthly Contribution: $_____**
- **Months to Goal: _____**
- **Target Date: _____**

Progress Tracker:

- January: $_____
- February: $_____
- March: $_____
- April: $_____
- May: $_____
- June: $_____
- July: $_____
- August: $_____
- September: $_____
- October: $_____
- November: $_____
- December: $_____
- **Total Saved: $_____**

Replenishment Plan:

- **Withdrawals: $_____ Date: _____**
- **New Monthly Contribution: $_____**

- **Adjusted Target Date:** _____

Educational Tips:

- **Saving Strategies:** _____
- **Importance of Liquidity:** _____
- **Review and Adjust:** _____

FINANCIAL BEHAVIOR SELF-ASSESSMENT TOOL

Now it's time for you to identify the cognitive biases and emotional triggers that influence your emotional decisions, particularly in the context of credit and debt management. With this, you can gain insights into your behavior and have a look at some strategies for making more informed financial choices.

Part 1: Questions

Understanding Your Financial Goals

What is your main financial goal?

A. Saving for a big purchase (e.g., house, car)
B. Paying off debt
C. Building an emergency fund
D. Investing for the future

Budgeting Habits

How often do you follow a budget?

A. Every month, without fail
B. Most months, but not always
C. Occasionally
D. I don't have a budget

How much of your income do you save or invest each month?

A. 20% or more
B. 10–19%
C. Less than 10%
D. I don't save or invest regularly

Debt Management

Which statement best describes your debt situation?

A. I have no debt.
B. I have manageable debt and make regular payments.
C. I struggle to keep up with my debt payments.
D. I am overwhelmed by debt.

How can you effectively manage the process of eliminating your debts?

A. I focus on paying off high-interest debts first.
B. I pay off the smallest debts first.

C. I pay whatever I can without a specific strategy.

D. I don't have a plan for debt repayment.

Savings and Investments

Do you have an emergency fund?

A. Yes, it covers 6+ months of expenses.

B. Yes, it covers 3–6 months of expenses.

C. Yes, but it covers less than 3 months of expenses.

D. No, I don't have an emergency fund.

How often do you review your investments?

A. Regularly, at least once a quarter

B. Occasionally, a few times a year

C. Rarely, maybe once a year

D. I don't have any investments

Financial Education and Knowledge

How do you rate your knowledge of personal finance?

A. High—I actively learn and stay informed.

B. Moderate—I know the basics but need more knowledge.

C. Low—I have limited knowledge and rarely seek out information.

D. Very low—I don't know much about personal finance.

How often do you seek out financial education resources?

A. Regularly—I read books, take courses, or consult experts.
B. Occasionally—I read articles or watch videos.
C. Rarely—I only look for help when I encounter a problem.
D. Never—I don't seek out financial education.

Credit Management

What is your current credit score?

A. Excellent (750+)
B. Good (700–749)
C. Fair (650–699)
D. Poor (below 650)

How often do you check your credit report?

A. At least once a year
B. Occasionally, when needed
C. Rarely, maybe once every few years
D. Never

Spending Habits

How often do you make impulsive purchases?

A. Rarely—I always plan and think carefully.
B. Sometimes—I occasionally buy on impulse.

C. Often—I struggle with controlling impulsive purchases.

D. Frequently—Most of my purchases are impulsive.

How do you approach major purchases?

A. I always research and compare prices.

B. I usually do some research but may not compare all options.

C. I rarely research or compare before buying.

D. I buy what I want without much thought.

Part 2: Interpreting Your Answers

1. Understanding Your Financial Goals

- **Mostly a/b:** You have clear financial goals and are actively working toward them.
- **Mostly c/d:** Consider focusing on defining and prioritizing your financial goals.

2. Budgeting Habits

- **Mostly a:** You have strong budgeting habits that support financial stability.
- **Mostly b:** Your budgeting is good, but there's some room for improvement.
- **Mostly c/d:** Creating and sticking to a budget will help you manage your finances better.

3. Debt Management

- **Mostly a/b:** You're managing your debt well.
- **Mostly c:** It's time to reassess your debt management strategy.
- **Mostly d:** Consider seeking help to tackle your debt effectively.

4. Savings and Investments

- **Mostly a:** You're well-prepared for emergencies and the future.
- **Mostly b/c:** You're on the right path but could improve your savings and investment habits.
- **Mostly d:** Prioritize building an emergency fund and exploring investment options.

5. Financial Education and Knowledge

- **Mostly a:** You're knowledgeable and proactive in managing your finances.
- **Mostly b:** You have a good foundation, but there's more to learn.
- **Mostly c/d:** Focus on improving your financial literacy to make better decisions.

6. Credit Management

- **Mostly a:** You have excellent credit management habits.
- **Mostly b:** You're doing well, but regular monitoring is key.
- **Mostly c/d:** Consider checking your credit report more often and working on improving your score.

7. Spending Habits

- **Mostly a:** You have disciplined spending habits.
- **Mostly b:** You're generally careful, but watch out for impulsive spending.
- **Mostly c/d:** Focus on controlling impulsive purchases and planning for major expenses.

Strategies for Improvement

- **Clarify and prioritize your financial goals:** Set specific, measurable goals and create a timeline for achieving them.
- **Strengthen your budgeting habits:** Use a budgeting app or spreadsheet to track income and expenses.
- **Enhance debt management:** Focus on paying off high-interest debts first and consider consolidation, if necessary.
- **Boost your savings and investments:** Automate your savings and invest regularly to build wealth over time.
- **Increase financial literacy:** Take advantage of free online courses, books, and financial planning tools.
- **Improve credit management:** Pay bills on time, reduce debt, and regularly monitor your credit score.
- **Manage spending habits:** Set limits on discretionary spending and avoid shopping without a list.

QUIZ #2: IDENTIFY YOUR COGNITIVE BIASES IN CREDIT MANAGEMENT

This quiz is designed to help you identify which cognitive biases might be influencing your credit behavior. With this, you can gain insights into your financial decision-making processes and learn strategies to counteract these biases, leading to better credit management.

1. When considering taking out a loan or applying for a new credit card, how do you approach the decision?

> A. I'm confident I can handle the payments, even if it means juggling multiple accounts.
> B. I focus on the benefits and assume that things will work out fine in the future.
> C. I'm most influenced by the initial offer or interest rate I see.
> D. I think about how others have successfully managed similar situations and feel reassured.

2. How do you manage your credit card balances?

> A. I often feel that I can handle multiple balances and plan to pay them off soon, but it doesn't always happen.
> B. I don't worry much about my balances because I expect my financial situation to improve.
> C. I signed up for the card because of the 0% interest rate offer and haven't thought much beyond that.

    D. I remember hearing about someone who easily
       paid off their credit card debt, so I believe I can
       do the same.

3. When it comes to paying bills, how do you prioritize your payments?

    A. I'm confident that I can manage all my
       payments without any issues.
    B. I don't worry much about paying off debt
       quickly because I assume I'll always have
       enough income to cover it.
    C. I focus on the payment with the lowest interest
       rate first because that was emphasized when I
       signed up.
    D. I think about how others have managed their
       bills successfully and use that as a guide.

4. How do you feel about your overall credit management strategy?

    A. I'm very confident in my ability to manage my
       credit effectively despite occasional challenges.
    B. I'm optimistic that my financial situation will
       improve, so I'm not too worried about my
       current credit usage.
    C. I tend to focus on initial credit terms and don't
       pay as much attention to the long-term impli-
       cations.
    D. I base my strategy on stories I've heard about
       others who have successfully managed their
       credit.

Scoring

Most a: Overconfidence Bias

- You tend to be confident in your financial abilities, which is great! However, be cautious of overestimating your capacity to manage multiple debts or complex credit situations. Consider reviewing your financial commitments regularly and ensure that you're not stretching yourself too thin.

Most b: Optimism Bias

- Your positive outlook is a strength, but you need to prepare for potential financial setbacks. Make sure you have a solid emergency fund and consider the "what ifs" when taking on new credit. Planning for the unexpected will help you maintain financial stability.

Most c: Anchoring

- You might be influenced by initial offers or interest rates when making credit decisions. While these can be attractive, be sure to look at the bigger picture. Review the extended conditions of your credit agreements and consider how changes in interest rates or other factors could impact your financial health.

Most d: Availability Heuristic

- It seems that you rely on stories or examples from others when making credit decisions. While learning from others' experiences is valuable, ensure that you're basing your decisions on a comprehensive understanding of *your* financial situation. Consider diversifying your information sources and making decisions that align with your unique financial goals.

GLOSSARY

Behavioral Economics: This discipline examines how psychological influences shape economic choices and financial behaviors.

Budgeting: This refers to developing a structured plan for distributing income among expenses, savings, and debt repayments to effectively manage personal finances.

Cash flow: The inflow and outflow of money within a person's financial framework.

Cognitive bias: These are systematic thinking errors that adversely impact financial decision-making, often resulting in illogical or less-than-optimal choices.

Compound interest: When money accrues interest on both the initial principal and the interest that has been added from previous periods.

Credit-builder loan: A modest loan created to assist people in establishing or enhancing their credit history through consistent payments.

Credit Bureau: This organization compiles and maintains credit data on people, supplying credit reports and scores to lenders.

Credit monitoring: The regular assessment of credit reports and scores to ensure financial wellness and identify potential issues early.

Credit report: A comprehensive account of a person's credit history, encompassing payment habits, outstanding debts, and public records.

Credit score: This numerical indicator reflects a person's credit-worthiness, utilized by lenders to gauge the likelihood of debt repayment.

Credit utilization: The ratio of used credit to available credit, which plays a crucial role in calculating a credit score.

Debt avalanche method: A strategy that focuses on paying down debts with the highest interest rates first to minimize overall interest expenditures.

Debt management: The approaches taken to effectively address and manage outstanding debts.

Debt snowball method: A repayment technique that prioritizes clearing the smallest debts first while maintaining minimum payments on larger obligations to build momentum.

Emergency budget: A temporary financial plan designed to adjust expenditures in response to unforeseen financial difficulties.

Emergency fund: A designated savings account aimed at covering unexpected costs or financial emergencies, typically suggested to cover three to six months of living expenses.

Financial goals: These are specific targets related to saving, investing, or spending money.

Financial literacy: This encompasses the knowledge necessary to understand financial concepts and tools, enabling informed and effective decision-making regarding financial resources.

Financial resilience: The capacity to rebound from financial challenges while maintaining a positive perspective amid difficulties.

Growth mindset: This belief holds that financial skills and capabilities can evolve through ongoing effort and education.

Income diversification: This practice involves cultivating multiple income sources instead of depending solely on a single stream.

Investing: Directing funds into assets with the anticipation of generating returns or profits over time.

Lifestyle inflation: This phenomenon occurs when increased earnings lead to greater spending, which can impede one's ability to save or invest effectively.

Loan terms: These details encompass the conditions associated with borrowing money, including interest rates, repayment schedules, and any applicable fees.

Mindful spending: This financial strategy emphasizes being fully conscious and deliberate about spending choices to align them with financial objectives.

Overconfidence bias: This trait involves overestimating one's financial competencies, resulting in risky behaviors such as accumulating excessive debt.

Passive income: This refers to revenue generated from investments or ventures that do not require daily management.

Philanthropy: The practice of contributing time, resources, or money to support charitable initiatives.

Present bias: A behavioral tendency that emphasizes immediate gratification over long-term benefits, often resulting in impulsive purchases and inadequate financial planning.

Retirement plan: This strategic financial approach aims to prepare for retirement, ensuring ample savings to sustain a desired lifestyle in later years.

Roth IRA: A type of retirement savings account that permits people to make contributions using after-tax income.

Savings rate: This metric represents the portion of income set aside for savings rather than expenditure.

Secured credit card: This credit card type requires a cash deposit as collateral, commonly used to establish or restore credit.

Tax planning: The process of assessing one's financial circumstances to minimize tax liabilities effectively.

RESOURCES FOR FURTHER READING

Books

- *Your Money or Your Life* by **Vicki Robin and Joe Dominguez:** A comprehensive guide to transforming your relationship with money and achieving financial independence.
- *The Total Money Makeover* by **Dave Ramsey:** A step-by-step plan for taking control of your finances, getting out of debt, and building wealth.
- *Nudge: Improving Decisions About Health, Wealth, and Happiness* by **Richard H. Thaler and Cass R. Sunstein:** Explores how behavioral economics can help individuals make better financial decisions.
- *The Intelligent Investor* by **Benjamin Graham:** A classic book on investing principles and long-term financial planning.

- *The Psychology of Money* by Morgan Housel: Offers timeless lessons on wealth, greed, and happiness, with a focus on the psychological aspects of financial behavior.
- *I Will Teach You to Be Rich* by Ramit Sethi: A practical guide to managing money, saving, and investing, with actionable advice on building wealth.

Articles

- **"The Role of Cognitive Biases in Financial Decision Making" by Daniel Kahneman:** An insightful article exploring how cognitive biases influence financial choices. You can find this article by searching for its title along with "Daniel Kahneman" on the *Harvard Business Review* website or through academic databases.
- **"Behavioral Economics: How Psychology Impacts Investing" by the CFA Institute:** An overview of how behavioral economics affects investment decisions and financial behavior. You can find this article by searching for it on the CFA Institute website or by looking up "Behavioral Economics" and "CFA Institute" together.
- **"Understanding Credit Scores" by the Consumer Financial Protection Bureau (CFPB):** A detailed explanation of how credit scores work and how they impact financial health. To find it, visit the CFPB's official website and search for "Understanding Credit Scores" in their resources section, or simply search for the title along with "CFPB" online.

Online Resources

1. **MyMoney.gov:** A U.S. government website that provides tools and resources for managing money, credit, and debt
2. **AnnualCreditReport.com:** The only authorized website to get your free annual credit reports from the three major credit bureaus
3. **Mint.com:** A personal finance management tool that helps track spending, create budgets, and monitor credit scores
4. **NerdWallet.com:** Offers a wealth of information on credit cards, loans, and personal finance, along with tools for comparing financial products
5. **Investopedia.com:** A comprehensive resource for financial education, including articles, tutorials, and a dictionary of financial terms

CONTACT INFORMATION FOR CREDIT COUNSELING AND FINANCIAL SUPPORT SERVICES

These resources and support services provide a strong foundation for continuing your education and seeking help when needed.

Clearpoint Credit Counseling Solutions (a division of Money Management International)

- **Website:** www.moneymanagement.org
- **Services:** Provides credit counseling, debt management plans, and housing counseling

Consumer Credit Counseling Service (CCCS)

- **Website:** www.consumercredit.com
- **Services:** Offers credit counseling, debt management plans, and financial education resources

The Consumer Financial Protection Bureau (CFPB)

- **Website:** www.consumerfinance.gov
- **Services:** Offers tools, resources, and information on credit, debt, and consumer financial rights

Credit.org

- **Website:** www.credit.org
- **Services:** Offers free financial education, credit counseling, and debt management services

Debt.org

- **Website:** www.debt.org
- **Services:** A resource for understanding and managing debt, offering connections to credit counseling services and educational content

Federal Trade Commission (FTC)

- **Website:** www.ftc.gov
- **Services:** Provides information on consumer rights, credit, and debt management, along with resources for reporting credit fraud

GreenPath Financial Wellness

- **Website:** www.greenpath.com
- **Services:** Provides credit counseling, debt management, housing counseling, and bankruptcy support

National Foundation for Credit Counseling (NFCC)

- **Website:** www.nfcc.org
- **Services:** Provides access to certified credit counselors who can help with debt management, budgeting, and financial education

REFERENCES

Ahmed, R. (2022). *How does the discovery of the uses for papyrus contribute to Egypt's development of civilization?* Quora. https://www.quora.com/How-does-the-discovery-of-the-uses-for-papyrus-contribute-to-Egypts-development-of-civilization

Akin, J. (2023, September 21). *What is Experian boost and how does it work?* Experian. https://www.experian.com/blogs/ask-experian/what-is-experian-boost-and-how-does-it-work/

Basha, S., Elgammal, M. & Abuzayed, B. (n.d.). *Online peer-to-peer lending: A review of the literature.* https://www.researchgate.net/publication/352452411_Online_Peer-To-Peer_Lending_A_Review_of_the_Literature

Black, M. (2021, March 8). *FICO vs. VantageScore credit scores: What's the difference?* Forbes Advisor. https://www.forbes.com/advisor/credit-score/fico-vs-vantagescore-credit-scores-whats-the-difference/

Chen, J. (2024, June 13). *Debt financing.* Investopedia. https://www.investopedia.com/terms/d/debtfinancing.asp

Clay tablets reveal accounting answers. (n.d.). Library of Congress, Washington. https://www.loc.gov/collections/cuneiform-tablets/articles-and-essays/clay-tablets-reveal-accounting-answers/

Clear, James. n.d. "How Long Does it Actually Take to Form a New Habit? (Backed by Science)." James Clear. Accessed September 4, 2024. https://jamesclear.com/new-habit

Consumer Resources. (n.d.). CFPB. https://www.consumerfinance.gov/consumer-tools/

Credit: What everyone should know. (2020). Investopedia. https://www.investopedia.com/terms/c/credit.asp

CreditBank PLC. (2023). *10 common financial mistakes to avoid in your 20s and 30s.* LinkedIn. https://www.linkedin.com/pulse/10-common-financial-mistakes-avoid-your-20s-30s-creditbankplc/

Credit scoring approaches guidelines. (2019). In World Bank Group. https://thedocs.worldbank.org/en/doc/935891585869698451-0130022020/original/CREDITSCORINGAPPROACHESGUIDELINESFINALWEB.pdf

Do other countries have credit scores? (2023). Capital One. https://www.capitalone.com/learn-grow/money-management/do-other-countries-have-credit-scores/

Dughi, P. (2019). *Do late payments affect my credit score?* Scored Credit. https://www.scoredcredit.com/late-payments-affect-credit-score

Egiyi, M. & Ogbodo, N. (2032). *Behavioral accounting: Analyzing how cognitive biases affect financial decisions and reporting.* https://www.researchgate.net/publication/ 373395320_Behavioral_Accounting_Analyzing_How_Cognitive_Biases_affect_Fi nancial_Decisions_and_Reporting

El Issa, E. (2024). *Do other countries have credit scores? - NerdWallet.* Nerdwallet. https://www.nerdwallet.com/article/finance/credit-score-canad-move-expat- country-abroad

Felix, H. & Hazard, J. (2019). *Roman law - The law of property and possession | Britannica.* In Encyclopædia Britannica. https://www.britannica.com/ topic/Roman-law/The-law-of-property-and-possession

Financial literacy and education commission. (2020, February 4). U.S. Department of the Treasury. https://home.treasury.gov/policy-issues/consumer-policy/finan cial-literacy-and-education-commission

Financial Pathways. (n.d.). *Retirement planning success stories.* Financial Pathways. https://www.financialpathways.net/retirement-wall-of-fame

Financial stress: The physical and mental effects. (2020, November 9). Quorum Federal Credit Union. https://www.quorumfcu.org/learn/money-management/finan cial-stress-the-physical-and-mental-effects/

Flanagan, G. L. (2022). *How a missed or late payment affects your credit score.* LendingTree. https://www.lendingtree.com/credit-repair/how-missed-or-late- payment-affects-credit/

Goodreads. n.d. "The Psychology of Money Quotes." Accessed September 4, 2024. https://www.goodreads.com/work/quotes/65374007-the-psychology-of-money

Gordon, J. S. (2023). *Andrew Carnegie and the Creation of U.S. Steel.* Bill of Rights Institute. https://billofrightsinstitute.org/essays/andrew-carnegie-and-the- creation-of-us-steel

Heakal, R. (2023, March 27). *What was the Glass-Steagall Act?* Investopedia. https:// www.investopedia.com/articles/03/071603.asp

Home. (n.d.). MyMoney.gov. https://www.mymoney.gov

Home page. (n.d.). Annual Credit Report. https://www.annualcreditreport.com

Hunt, J. (2023, October 6). *How to stay motivated when paying off debt.* Credit Counselling Society. https://nomoredebts.org/blog/dealing-with-debt/how-to- stay-motivated-when-paying-off

Importance of cash reserves. (n.d.). Faster Capital. https://fastercapital.com/startup- topic/Importance-of-Cash-Reserves.html

leahhalll. (2022). *Microeconomics final exam.* Quizlet. https://quizlet.com/776225512/ microeconomics-final-exam-flash-cards/

Makhado, P. (2023, November 5). *The limitations of traditional credit scoring systems.* Medium. https://medium.com/@phindulo60/the-limitations-of-traditional- credit-scoring-systems-e92833fdfa8a

Mwelwa, D. (2023). *Unveiling the renaissance: A remarkable journey of banking and financial revolution*. Www.linkedin.com. https://www.linkedin.com/pulse/unveiling-renaissance-remarkable-journey-banking-financial-mwelwa/

Natonwide. (n.d.). *What are financial assets?* Nationwide. https://nationwide.com/lc/resources/personal-finance/articles/types-ofassets

Norris, E. (2022, June 14). *Top 10 most common financial mistakes*. Investopedia. https://www.investopedia.com/personalfinance/most-common-financial-mistakes/

Northup, G. (2023, March 29). *10 ways to Increase your current income*. Indeed Career Guide. https://www.indeed.com/careeradvice/starting-new-job/how-increase-income

Nova, A. (2024, February 16). *After 35 years, he got $119,500 in student debt forgiven. Then the government refunded him $56,801*. CNBC. https://www.cnbc.com/2024/02/16/he-got-his-student-debt-forgiven-and-then-a-56801-refund.html

O'Shea, B. & Pyles, S. (2024). *How to use debt avalanche*. NerdWallet. https://www.nerdwallet.com/article/finance/what-is-adebt-avalanche

PRBA. (n.d.). *Can you have a credit card without a credit score? can you have a credit card without a credit score?* https://www.prba.net/best-credit-cards/can-you-have-a-credit-card-without-a-credit-score

Preparing for the unexpected. (n.d.). Securities.sos.in.gov. https://securities.sos.in.gov/moneywise/budgeting/preparing-for-theunexpected/

Ramsey. (2024). *How to increase your income*. Ramsey Solutions. https://www.ramseysolutions.com/saving/how-to-increaseyour-income

Recover from a financial setback. (n.d.). Bannerbank. https://www.bannerbank.com/financial-resources/blog/5-steps-to-help-yourecover-from-a-financial-setback

Schwahn, L. (2023, July 18). *Financial goals: Definition and examples*. NerdWallet. https://www.nerdwallet.com/article/finance/financial-goals-definition-example

Segal, T. (2023). *What is diversification? Definition as an investing strategy*. Investopedia. https://www.investopedia.com/terms/d/diversification.asp#toc-diversification-strategies

Silver, C. (2022, February 3). *The ultimate guide to financial literacy*. Investopedia. https://www.investopedia.com/guide-tofinancial-literacy-4800530

SimplePath. (2023). *The benefits of tracking your spending habits and how to do it*. LinkedIn. https://www.linkedin.com/pulse/benefits-tracking-your-spending-habits-how-do-thesimplepath/

Stevens, M. (2014). *Economic decision-making and money-making strategies in Ancient Greece*. https://deepblue.lib.umich.edu/bitstream/handle/2027.42/107319/leesemic_1.pdf

The transcontinental railroad. (2022, February 6). American Battlefield Trust. https://www.battlefields.org/learn/articles/transcontinental-railroad

What is financial forecasting + how to do it [7 Steps]. (n.d.). Paddle. https://www.paddle.com/resources/financial-forecasting

White, J. (2019, May 30). *Importance of establishing credit when young - Experian*. Experian. https://www.experian.com/blogs/ask-experian/why-it-is-important-to-establish-credit-when-you-are-young/

www.ingramcontent.com/pod-product-compliance
Lightning Source LLC
Chambersburg PA
CBHW031852200326
41597CB00012B/385